FREE VIDEO

FREE VIDEO

Essential Test Tips Video from Trivium Test Prep!

Dear Customer,

Thank you for purchasing from Trivium Test Prep! We're honored to help you prepare for your exam.

To show our appreciation, we're offering a **FREE *Essential Test Tips* Video by Trivium Test Prep**.* Our video includes 35 test preparation strategies that will make you successful on your exam. All we ask is that you email us your feedback and describe your experience with our product. Amazing, awful, or just so-so: we want to hear what you have to say!

To receive your **FREE *Essential Test Tips* Video**, please email us at 5star@triviumtestprep.com. Include "Free 5 Star" in the subject line and the following information in your email:

1. The title of the product you purchased.
2. Your rating from 1 – 5 (with 5 being the best).
3. Your feedback about the product, including how our materials helped you meet your goals and ways in which we can improve our products.
4. Your full name and shipping address so we can send your **FREE *Essential Test Tips* Video**.

If you have any questions or concerns please feel free to contact us directly at: 5star@ triviumtestprep.com.

Thank you!

– Trivium Test Prep Team

*To get access to the free video please email us at 5star@triviumtestprep.com, and please follow the instructions above.

IELTS Academic Exam Prep:

STUDY GUIDE WITH AUDIO AND PRACTICE QUESTIONS
FOR THE INTERNATIONAL
ENGLISH LANGUAGE TESTING SYSTEM EXAM,
ALL SUBJECTS

ELISSA SIMON

TABLE OF CONTENTS

INTRODUCTION

Congratulations on choosing to take the IELTS Academic (IELTS-A)! By purchasing this book, you've taken an important step on your academic career in the English-speaking world.

This guide will provide you with a detailed overview of the IELTS-A so that you know exactly what to expect on test day. We'll take you through all the concepts covered on the assessments and give you the opportunity to test your knowledge with practice questions. Even if it's been a while since you last took a major test, don't worry; we'll make sure you're more than ready!

WHAT IS THE IELTS-A?

The IELTS-A measures a candidate's English-language ability for advanced academic study. It tests and affirms English reading, writing, speaking, and listening abilities at the undergraduate and postgraduate levels.

WHAT'S ON THE IELTS-A?

The exam is composed of four tests: Listening, Reading, Writing, and Speaking. Candidates must take the Listening, Reading, and Writing tests on the same day. These three tests may be administered in any order. The Speaking test may be administered on the same day or on a different day.

What's on the IELTS-A?

TEST	TOPICS	NUMBER OF QUESTIONS	TIME
Listening	■ a conversation in a social context ■ a monologue in a social context ■ a conversation among multiple people in an educational context ■ a monologue on an academic topic ■ Each recording is followed by various question types to test for comprehension (e.g., filling out a diagram, fill-in-the-blank, multiple choice, true or false, short answer).	40	30 minutes

TEST	TOPICS	NUMBER OF QUESTIONS	TIME
Reading	■ 3 articles or excerpts from books, magazines, or newspapers on academic topics of general interest at the undergraduate level (total text length is 2,150 – 2,750 words) ■ Each section is followed by various question types to test for comprehension (e.g., filling out a diagram, fill-in-the-blank, multiple choice, true or false, short answer).	40	60 minutes
Writing	■ Task 1: Review and describe visual data (e.g., graph, diagram, chart) ■ Task 2: Write an essay responding to a certain perspective or evaluating and challenging an argument	2 tasks	60 minutes
Speaking	■ a live, three-part interview with another individual in English ■ Part 1: general introduction with the interviewer (4 – 5 minutes) ■ Part 2: individual long-turn on a topic chosen by the interviewer (3 – 4 minutes) ■ Part 3: a two-way discussion with the interviewer on the topic raised in Part 2 (4 – 5 minutes)	–	11 – 14 minutes
Total		82 and interview	Approximately 2 hours and 45 minutes

HOW IS THE IELTS-A SCORED?

You cannot pass or fail the IELTS. Instead, your results are reported as "band scores" on a scale of 1 (the lowest) to 9 (the highest).

On the Listening and Reading tests, you will receive one point for each question you answer correctly out of the 40 questions. Those points are converted to the band scores. For example, a candidate who answers all 40 questions correctly on the Reading test will receive a score of 9. A candidate who answers 35 questions correctly on the Listening test will receive a score of 8. Details on conversion from raw scores to band scores can be found at ielts.org/criteria.

On the Writing test, examiners will take into account IELTS Writing test assessment criteria. These include Task Achievement/Response (whether you fulfilled the task and answered the question), Coherence and Cohesion (clarity of writing), Lexical Resource (vocabulary), and Grammatical Range and Accuracy (appropriate use of grammar). The examiners will convert their analysis into a band score on the 1 – 9 scale. Details on the Writing test criteria are found at ielts.org/criteria.

On the Speaking test, examiners use IELTS Speaking test assessment criteria. These include Fluency and Coherence (flow of speech), Lexical Resource (vocabulary), Grammatical Range and Accuracy (appropriate use of grammar), and Pronunciation. The examiners will convert their analysis into a band score on the 1 – 9 scale. Details on the Speaking test criteria are found at ielts.org/criteria.

How is the IELTS-A Administered?

The IELTS is administered on Saturdays and Thursdays, four times a month, at testing sites around the world. To find the closest test center near you and register for a test, check ielts.org.

On test day, arrive early. Check with the facility and ielts.org to make sure you know what type of identification to bring (usually government-issued photo identification). Personal belongings, cell phones, and other electronic, photographic, recording, or listening devices are not permitted in the testing center. Many testing centers offer lockers to secure your personal items, but you should check with the facility beforehand to find out if storage is available.

About This Guide

This guide will help you master the most important test topics and develop critical test-taking skills. We have built features into our books to prepare you for your tests and increase your score. Along with a detailed summary of the test's format, content, and scoring, we offer an in-depth overview of the content knowledge required to score high on your IELTS. In the review, you'll find sidebars that provide interesting information, highlight key concepts, and review content so that you can solidify your understanding of important concepts. You can also test your knowledge with sample questions throughout the text and with practice questions. We're pleased you've chosen Trivium to be a part of your journey!

LISTENING AND SPEAKING

INTRO TO IELTS-A LISTENING

What's on the IELTS-A Listening?

The listening portion of the IELTS will consist of forty questions and lasts approximately thirty minutes, not including the ten minutes allowed to transfer answers into the answer booklet. The questions on the listening portion of the test are in several formats:

- multiple choice
- matching
- map/diagram labeling
- form completion
- note completion
- table/flow-chart completion
- summary completion
- sentence completion
- short answer

The test is divided into four sections. The first section is a CONVERSATION BETWEEN TWO PEOPLE THAT HAS A SOCIAL CONTEXT. The second section is a MONOLOGUE WITH A SOCIAL CONTEXT. Social contexts are conversations not related to work, school, or academics. They are generally conversations or speeches a person might hear in his or her everyday life. Some examples might be a conversation about purchasing an insurance policy, a conversation with a health care provider, a monologue given by the tour guide at a museum, or a speech given to welcome attendees at an event.

The third section is a CONVERSATION AMONG UP TO FOUR PEOPLE ABOUT SOMETHING RELATED TO EDUCATION OR TRAINING. The discussion might be about selecting classes for a degree program or how to handle a challenging assignment. The final section is a MONOLOGUE ON AN ACADEMIC SUBJECT. This might be a lesson or lecture presented by a teacher, professor, or someone similar.

Vocabulary in all four sections will often focus on wants, needs, preferences, and requirements, so associated terms should be expected on the exam and therefore practiced. Vocabulary associated with common settings (e.g., auto repair shop, doctor's office, restaurant, school registrar's office, tutoring center, and so forth) should also be practiced and expected. Monologues and dialogues will focus on events in the past, present, and future, so examinees should expect to hear many different verb tenses.

Examinees should also be prepared to hear multiple accents and voices. Speakers will include men, women, young people, older people, and both native and non-native English speakers with accents from various regions.

The test will assess not only an overall understanding of what is said but also an understanding of main ideas and the specific points made by speakers and their overall attitudes.

Each section will be played only one time.

Tips for the IELTS-A Listening Section

To prepare for the IELTS listening portion, one should listen to as many conversations and monologues as possible. Additionally, test-takers should consider the various opportunities to hear English being spoken in similar contexts. Such situations include:

- television programs;
- online videos (e.g., YouTube);
- radio programs and podcasts;
- audio recordings of speeches or audio books; and
- audio- or video-recorded lectures or lessons by teachers or professors.

It is also very helpful to practice writing down spoken words. Since spelling and grammar mistakes do count on the exam, it is important to be able to record words and phrases correctly.

INTRO TO IELTS-A SPEAKING

What's on the IELTS-A Speaking?

The speaking portion of the IELTS is divided into three parts. Part One will generally last around four to five minutes. During this **INTRODUCTORY INTERVIEW**, the examiner will make introductions and ask general questions. These questions will typically focus on individual circumstances and interests. The examinee should be prepared to answer questions about:

- family (e.g., spouse, siblings, parents)
- hobbies/interests (e.g., sports, activities)
- future plans (e.g., school, work)
- other familiar topics (e.g., the day's weather, the temperature of the room)

Part Two will last three to four minutes and is referred to as **LONG TURN**. In this portion, examinees are given a **TASK CARD**. The task card specifies the topic about which the examinee will speak. After the task card is received, examinees are given one minute to write down notes to prepare the talk. Examinees will then speak for one to two minutes on the topic assigned by the task card. After the talk, the examiner may ask one or two questions based on the topic from the task card.

Part three is a **TWO-WAY DISCUSSION** that will last four to five minutes. During this discussion, the examiner and the examinee will discuss abstract ideas and issues related to the topic from the task card. The examiner will lead the discussion with open-ended questions, but examinees will need to be ready to provide robust and well-considered responses.

Scoring on this portion of the exam is based on overall English-speaking skills as well as the ability to organize ideas, state opinions, and support those statements. The examinee's opinions themselves are NOT part of the score on the exam.

Vocabulary related to personal feelings and beliefs as well as basic transitional phrases (e.g., *also*, *additionally*, *furthermore*, and so forth) are important in the speaking section. Command of all verb tenses is also critical since discussions may focus on topics or beliefs about events or situations of the past, present, or future.

Tips for the IELTS-A Speaking Section

Practicing for the speaking section of the exam requires examinees to do a lot of talking! Having frequent conversations in English is certainly helpful. In such conversations, it is a good idea to practice stating opinions or preferences and explaining the "why" behind them. It is also helpful to practice using a variety of verb tenses and switching between these tenses as the conversation requires.

To practice for the long turn speech, examinees do not need a partner. They do, however, need to practice speaking about a variety of topics and can use video or audio to record themselves or even practice in front of a mirror. Some suggestions for speaking practice include:

- events attended (e.g., musical performances, plays, festivals);
- past positive experiences (e.g., helping others, when others have helped you);
- large projects or events with which you have been involved;
- teams or groups of which you have been a member;
- things you have learned (e.g., skills, hobbies, teamwork);
- challenges you have overcome;
- people you know;
- customs/celebrations/food from your country of origin; and
- things you like/dislike about technology.

When practicing, you must be sure to time each speech and aim to speak for two minutes.

Keep in mind that the examiner will evaluate speakers on language skills, not opinions. Don't worry about trying to "please" or "agree with" the examiner—this will cause unnecessary anxiety! Focus on preparing to speak on a wide variety of topics, even those which are unfamiliar.

It is also wise to practice using **FILLERS**, or **HESITATION DEVICES**. These are words or phrases that effectively create brief moments of time for thinking about what to say next. Some common examples are:

- That's a good question.
- Let me think about that.
- That's an interesting question.
- I'll have to think about that for a minute.
- Well . . .
- You see . . .
- So, basically . . .

READING

The reading questions on the IELTS-A focus on **ACADEMIC READING**. The Academic Reading section has three passages with forty questions in total. The texts will address issues of general knowledge. They are taken from articles, books, and journals. You do not need any background knowledge to answer the questions beyond what is provided in the readings. You may need to interpret visual images like diagrams or graphs.

Questions may address anything from the main idea of the passage, vocabulary words in the passage, the author's message or intention, and more. Questions are presented in a variety of formats, including multiple choice, sentence completion, and identifying information in the text.

This chapter will review key concepts in reading comprehension to help you prepare for the exam.

THE MAIN IDEA

The **TOPIC** is a word or short phrase that explains what a passage is about. The **MAIN IDEA** is a complete sentence that explains what the author is trying to say about the topic. Generally, the **TOPIC SENTENCE** is the first (or near the first) sentence in a paragraph. It is a general statement that introduces the topic so that the reader knows what to expect.

The **SUMMARY SENTENCE**, on the other hand, frequently (but not always!) comes at the end of a paragraph or passage because it wraps up all the ideas presented. This sentence summarizes what an author has said about the topic. Some passages, particularly short ones, will not include a summary sentence.

> ✔ To find the main idea, identify the topic and then ask, "What is the author trying to tell me about the topic?"

Table 2.1. Identifying the Topic and Main Idea

The cisco, a foot-long freshwater fish native to the Great Lakes, once thrived throughout the basin but had virtually disappeared by the 1950s. However, today fishermen are pulling them up by the net-load in Lake Michigan and Lake Ontario. It is highly unusual for a native species to revive, and the reason for the cisco's reemergence is even more unlikely. The cisco have an invasive species—quagga mussels—to thank for their return. Quagga mussels depleted nutrients in the lakes, harming other species highly dependent on these nutrients. Cisco, however, thrive in low-nutrient environments. As other species—many of which were invasive—diminished, cisco flourished in their place.

TOPIC SENTENCE	The cisco, a foot-long freshwater fish native to the Great Lakes, once thrived throughout the basin but had virtually disappeared by the 1950s.
TOPIC	cisco
SUMMARY SENTENCE	As other species—many of which were invasive—diminished, cisco flourished in their place.
MAIN IDEA	Cisco had nearly disappeared from the lake but now flourish thanks to the invasive quagga mussel.

Practice Questions

1. Tourists flock to Yellowstone National Park each year to view the geysers that bubble and erupt throughout it. What most of these tourists do not know is that these geysers are formed by a caldera—a hot crater in the earth's crust—which was created by a series of three eruptions of an ancient super volcano. These eruptions, which began 2.1 million years ago, spewed between 1,000 to 2,450 cubic kilometers of volcanic matter at such a rate that the volcano's magma chamber collapsed, creating the craters.

   What is the topic of the passage?

   A) tourists

   B) geysers

   C) volcanic eruptions

   D) super volcanos

2. The Battle of Little Bighorn, commonly called Custer's Last Stand, was a battle between the Lakota, the Northern Cheyenne, the Arapaho, and the Seventh Cavalry Regiment of the US Army. Led by war leaders Crazy Horse and Chief Gall and the religious leader Sitting Bull, the allied tribes of the Plains Indians decisively defeated their US foes. Two hundred and sixty-eight US soldiers were killed, including General George Armstrong Custer, two of his brothers, his nephew, his brother-in-law, and six Indian scouts.

   What is the main idea of this passage?

   A) Most of General Custer's family died in the Battle of Little Bighorn.

   B) The Seventh Cavalry regiment was formed to fight Native American tribes.

   C) Sitting Bull and George Custer were fierce enemies.

   D) The Battle of Little Bighorn was a significant victory for the Plains Indians.

SUPPORTING DETAILS

Statements that describe or explain the main idea are SUPPORTING DETAILS. Supporting details are often found after the topic sentence. They support the main idea through examples, descriptions, and explanations.

Authors may add details to support their argument or claim. FACTS are details that point to truths, while OPINIONS are based on personal beliefs or judgments. To differentiate between fact and opinion, look for statements that express feelings, attitudes, or beliefs that can't be proven (opinions) and statements that can be proven (facts).

> ⚠ To find supporting details, look for sentences that connect to the main idea and tell more about it.

Table 2.2. Supporting Details and Fact and Opinion

Bait is an important element of fishing. Some people use live bait, such as worms and night crawlers. Others use artificial bait, such as lures and spinners. Live bait has a scent that fish are drawn to. Live bait is a good choice for fishing. It's cheap and easy to find. Lures can vibrate, make noise, and mimic the movements of some fish. People should choose artificial bait over live bait because it can be used multiple times.

SUPPORTING DETAILS	Lures can vibrate, make noise, and mimic the movements of some fish.
FACT	Live bait has a scent that fish are drawn to.
OPINION	Live bait is a good choice for fishing.

Practice Questions

3. Increasingly, companies are turning to subcontracting services rather than hiring full-time employees. This provides companies with advantages like greater flexibility, reduced legal responsibility to employees, and lower possibility of unionization within the company. However, this has led to increasing confusion and uncertainty over the legal definition of employment. Courts have grappled with questions about the hiring company's responsibility in maintaining fair labor practices. Companies argue that they delegate that authority to subcontractors, while unions and other worker-advocate groups argue that companies still have a legal obligation to the workers who contribute to their business.

   Which detail BEST supports the idea that using contract employees is beneficial to companies?

   A) Uncertainty over the legal definition of employment increases.

   B) Companies still have a legal obligation to contractors.

   C) There is a lower possibility of unionization within the company.

   D) Contractors, not companies, control fair labor practices.

4. Chalk is a colorful way for kids and adults to have fun and be creative. Chalk is used on playgrounds and sidewalks. Children love to draw pictures in different colors. The designs are beautiful, but they are also messy. Chalk doesn't clean up easily. It has to wash away. Chalk is also used by cafés and bakeries. Shops use chalk to showcase their menus and special items. It is a great way to advertise their food.

Which statement from the passage is an opinion?

A) It is a great way to advertise their food.

B) Chalk doesn't clean up easily.

C) It has to wash away.

D) Shops use chalk to showcase their menus and special items.

DRAWING CONCLUSIONS

> Look for facts, character actions and dialogue, how each sentence connects to the topic, and the author's reasoning for an argument when drawing conclusions.

Readers can use information that is EXPLICIT, or clearly stated, along with information that is IMPLICIT, or indirect, to make inferences and DRAW CONCLUSIONS. Readers can determine meaning from what is implied by using details, context clues, and prior knowledge. When answering questions, consider what is known from personal experiences and make note of all information the author has provided before drawing a conclusion.

Table 2.3. Drawing Conclusions

When the Spanish-American War broke out in 1898, the US Army was small and understaffed. President William McKinley called for 1,250 volunteers to serve in the First US Volunteer Calvary. The ranks were quickly filled by cowboys, gold prospectors, hunters, gamblers, Native Americans, veterans, police officers, and college students looking for an adventure. The officer corps was composed of veterans of previous wars. With more volunteers than it could accept, the army set high standards: all the recruits had to be skilled on horseback and with guns. Consequently, they became known as the Rough Riders.

QUESTION	Why are the volunteers named Rough Riders?
EXPLICIT INFORMATION	Different people volunteered, men were looking for adventure, and recruits had to be extremely skilled on horseback and with guns due to a glut of volunteers.
IMPLICIT INFORMATION	Men had previous occupations, officer corps veterans worked with volunteers.
CONCLUSION DRAWN	The men were called Rough Riders because they were inexperienced yet particularly enthusiastic to help with the war and were willing to put in extra effort to join.

Practice Question

5. After World War I, political and social forces pushed for a return to normalcy in the United States. The result was disengagement from the larger world and increased focus on American economic growth and personal enjoyment. Caught in the middle were American writers, raised on the values of the prewar world and frustrated with what they viewed as the superficiality and materialism of postwar American culture. Many of them fled to Paris, where they became known as the "lost generation," creating a trove of literary works criticizing their home culture and delving into their own feelings of alienation.

   Which conclusion about the effects of war is most likely true?

   A) War served as an inspiration for literary works.

   B) It was difficult to stabilize countries after war occurred.

   C) Writers were torn between supporting war and their own ideals.

   D) Individual responsibility and global awareness declined after the war.

THE AUTHOR'S PURPOSE AND POINT OF VIEW

The **AUTHOR'S PURPOSE** is an author's reason for writing a text. Authors may write to share an experience, entertain, persuade, or inform readers. This can be done through persuasive, expository, and narrative writing.

PERSUASIVE WRITING influences the actions and thoughts of readers. Authors state an opinion, then provide reasons that support the opinion. **EXPOSITORY WRITING** outlines and explains steps in a process. Authors focus on a sequence of events. **NARRATIVE WRITING** tells a story. Authors include a setting, plot, characters, problem, and solution in the text.

Authors also share their **POINT OF VIEW** (perspectives, attitudes, and beliefs) with readers. Identify the author's point of view by word choice, details, descriptions, and characters' actions. The author's attitude or **TONE** can be found in word choice that conveys feelings or stance on a topic.

> Use the acronym P.I.E.S.—*persuade*, *inform*, *entertain*, *state*—to help you remember elements of an author's purpose.

TEXT STRUCTURE is the way the author organizes a text. A text can be organized to show a problem and solution, compare and contrast, or even investigate cause and effect. Structure of a text can give insight into an author's purpose and point of view. If a text is organized to pose an argument or advertise a product, it can be considered persuasive. The author's point of view will be revealed in how thoughts and opinions are expressed in the text.

Table 2.4. The Author's Purpose and Point of View

Superfoods are foods that are found in nature. They are rich in nutrients and low in calories. Many people are concerned about healthy diets and weight loss, so superfoods are a great meal choice! The antioxidants and vitamins found in superfoods decrease the risk of diseases and aid in heart health.

AUTHOR'S PURPOSE	persuade readers of the benefit of superfoods
POINT OF VIEW	advocates superfoods as "a great meal choice"
TONE	positive, encouraging, pointing out the benefits of superfoods, using positive words like *great* and *rich*
STRUCTURE	cause and effect to show the results of eating superfoods

Practice Questions

6. University of California, Berkeley, researchers decided to tackle an age-old problem: why shoelaces come untied. They recorded the shoelaces of a volunteer walking on a treadmill by attaching devices to record the acceleration, or g-force, experienced by the knot. The results were surprising. A shoelace knot experiences more g-force from a person walking than any rollercoaster can generate. However, if the person simply stomped or swung their feet—the two movements that make up a walker's stride—the g-force was not enough to undo the knots.

   What is the purpose of this passage?

   A) to confirm if shoelaces always come undone

   B) to compare the force of treadmills and rollercoasters

   C) to persuade readers to tie their shoes tighter

D) to describe the results of an experiment on shoelaces

7. What do you do with plastic bottles? Do you throw them away, or do you recycle or reuse them? As landfills continue to fill up, there will eventually be no place to put our trash. If you recycle or reuse bottles, you will help reduce waste and turn something old into a creative masterpiece!

Which of the following BEST describes what the author believes?

A) Landfills are unnecessary.

B) Reusing objects requires creativity.

C) Recycling helps the environment.

D) Reusing objects is better than recycling.

8. Negative cinematic representations of gorillas have provoked fear and contribute to hunting practices that endanger gorilla populations. It's a shame that many films portray them as scary and aggressive creatures. Their size and features should not be cause for alarm. Gorillas are actually shy and act aggressively only when provoked.

What can be inferred about the author's attitude toward gorillas?

A) The author is surprised that people do not know the truth about gorillas.

B) The author is concerned that movies distort people's opinion of gorillas.

C) The author is saddened by the decrease in gorilla populations.

D) The author is afraid that gorillas are being provoked.

9.

Want smoother skin? Try Face Lace, a mix of shea butter and coconut oil. Like most creams it is soft and easy to apply. We rank #1 in sales and free trials. Our competitor Smooth Moves may be great for blemishes, but we excel at reducing the signs of aging!

What is the structure of this text?

A) cause and effect

B) order and sequence

C) problem and solution

D) compare and contrast

TEXT FEATURES

TEXT FEATURES are components of a text that include information that is not in the main text. They help readers determine what is essential in a text and show where to find key information. Before reading, look at the text features to get an understanding of what a text is about.

Text features help readers increase background knowledge and learn new information.

HEADINGS and SUBHEADINGS show how information is organized and help readers identify the main points of each section in a text.

FOOTNOTES are notes at the bottom of a page that reference or cite information, definitions, explanations, or comments.

Text features such as ITALICS and BOLDFACE are used for emphasis. Italicized words appear slanted and signify titles, scientific terms, footnote references, and emphasized words. Boldface print makes words stand out from the rest of the text on a page and draws the reader's attention. It is used to highlight ideas, introduce new vocabulary, or emphasize main points.

The TABLE OF CONTENTS and INDEX are text features that help organize information. The table of contents shows a book's structure, outlining its sections and chapters. An index consists of a list of words and phrases in alphabetical order that outlines various topics in a book. Page numbers are provided to guide readers to sections of the book.

Table 2.5. Text Features

CHAPTER TWO: RATTLESNAKES

Rattlesnake Habitats

There are 13 species (*crotalus* or *sistrurus*) of rattlesnakes. Rattlesnakes adapt to different **habitats**. They can live in deserts, meadows, or swamps. Rocky crevices are great places to hide and make dens.

Keeping Predators Away

Rattlesnakes have a rattle at the base of their tails. The vibrations of the rattle deter **predators**. Hissing sounds are also a warning to other animals. Other ways to ward off predators include coiling their bodies and raising their heads in order to strike and bite.[1]

[1] Some rattlesnakes camouflage themselves to avoid predators.

BOLDING	habitats, predators
ITALICS	crotalus, sistrurus
HEADING/SUBHEADING	Chapter Two: Rattlesnakes/Rattlesnake Habitats, Keeping Predators Away
FOOTNOTE	Some rattlesnakes camouflage themselves to avoid predators.

Practice Questions

10.

INDEX

B
basic operation....7
battery..................7

C
call log 9
cell phone.............7
contacts................9
cordless phones ..6

D
delete info 9
dialing numbers ..9

H
handset 10

I
installation 7
Internet..................8

L
landline 5

M
memory card........8

P
pay phone 6

R
receiver..................5
ringtone 9
rotary phone.........5

S
SIM card.................9
smartphone 7

T
text message 10
touch screen.........9

V
voicemail..............10

W
WiFi 8
wireless network ..8

What inference can be made about this book based on its index?

A) The book is about different types of phones.

B) The book is about modern-day mobile phones.

C) The book is about the history of cell phones.

D) The book is about how to contact someone via phone.

11. Popular stories like *The Three Little Pigs* are often retold and changed into what are known as *twisted* fairy tales. *The Three Little Javelinas* is a tale similar to *The Three Little Pigs*, but it has a different setting and characters. It takes place in a desert instead of a forest, and the javelinas outsmart a coyote instead of a wolf.

Italics are used in the text to indicate which of the following?

A) titles and references to footnotes

B) foreign phrases

C) emphasized words and titles

D) scientific terms

MEANING OF WORDS

To understand the meanings of unfamiliar words, use **CONTEXT CLUES**. Context clues are hints the author provides to help readers define difficult words. They can be found in words or phrases in the same sentence or in a neighboring sentence. Look for synonyms, antonyms, definitions, examples, and explanations in the text to determine the meaning of the unfamiliar word.

Sometimes parts of a word can make its meaning easier to determine. **AFFIXES** are added to **ROOT WORDS** (a word's basic form) to modify meaning. **PREFIXES** are added to the beginning of root words, while **SUFFIXES** are added to the ending. Divide words into parts, finding meaning in each part. Take, for example, the word *unjustifiable*: the prefix is *un–* (*not*), the root word is *justify* ("to prove reasonable"), and the suffix is *–able* ("referring to a quality").

> ⚠️
> Use what you know about a word to figure out its meaning, then look for clues in the sentence or paragraph.

Another way to determine the meaning of unknown words is to consider their denotation and connotation with other words in the sentence. **DENOTATION** is the literal meaning of a word, while **CONNOTATION** is the positive or negative associations of a word.

Authors use words to convey thoughts, but the meaning may be different from the literal meaning of the words. This is called **FIGURATIVE LANGUAGE**. Types of figurative language include similes, metaphors, hyperboles, and personification.

Similes compare two things that are not alike with the words *like* or *as*. Metaphors are used to compare two things that are not exactly alike but may share a certain characteristic.

Hyperboles are statements that exaggerate something in order to make a point or draw attention to a certain feature. Personification involves using human characteristics to describe an animal or object.

Table 2.6. Meanings of Words

Have you ever gone to a flea market? There are rows of furniture, clothing, and antiques waiting for discovery. Unlike a museum with items on display, flea markets are opportunities to learn and shop. Vendors bring their handmade goods to this communal event to show their crafts and make money.

CONTEXT CLUES	Vendors are people who sell things; people shop at a flea market.
AFFIXES	The prefix *com–* in *communal* means *with* or *together*.
MEANING	*Communal* means "shared with a community."

Practice Questions

12. The Bastille, Paris's famous historical prison, was originally built in 1370 as a fortification—called a *bastide* in Old French—to protect the city from English invasion. It rose 100 feet into the air, had eight towers, and was surrounded by a moat more than eighty feet wide. In the seventeenth century, the government **converted** the fortress into an elite prison for upper-class felons, political disruptors, and spies.

    Which word or phrase can be used to determine the meaning of *converted*?

    A) originally built

    B) fortification

    C) felons

    D) historical prison

13. Breaking a world record is no easy feat. An application and video submission of an amazing skill may not be enough. Potential record breakers may need to demonstrate their skill in front of an official world records judge. The judge will watch a performance of a record attempt to determine if the record-breaking claim is **credible**. After all evidence is collected, reviewed, and approved, a certificate for the new world record is granted!

    Based on affixes and context clues, what does *credible* mean?

    A) believable

    B) achievable

    C) likeable

    D) noticeable

14. Every year people gather in Durham Park to participate in the Food Truck Rodeo. A band plays, and the food trucks are like a carnival of delicious treats. The aroma of food draws all who pass by, creating a large crowd. The event is free to attend; patrons pay only for what they want to eat. From pizzas and burgers to hotdogs and pastries, there's something for everyone!

    Which type of figurative language is used in the second sentence?

    A) hyperbole

    B) metaphor

    C) personification

    D) simile

FOLLOWING DIRECTIONS AND RECOGNIZING SEQUENCES

When following a set of directions, look for **SIGNAL WORDS** that indicate steps of a process. These words will tell you when things need to happen in a certain order. Signal words should show a transition from one event or step to another.

⚠️

To find signal words, ask, *What happened first and what happened after that?*

When reading a passage, you will find that signal words can be used to follow the direction of the author's ideas and the sequence of events. Signal words show time order and how details flow in a chronological way.

Table 2.7. Following Directions and Recognizing Sequences

NASA wanted to launch a man from Earth to the moon. At first NASA used satellites for launch tests. Then in June of 1968, astronauts aboard the Apollo 8 launched into space and circled the moon ten times before returning to Earth. Finally, in 1969 three astronauts reached the moon in the Apollo 11 spacecraft. After a successful landing, two members of the crew walked on the moon. During their walk, they collected data and samples of rocks. They returned as heroes of space exploration.

signal words	*At first, Then, Finally, After, During*

Practice Questions

15.

> **FANTASTIC HARD-BOILED EGGS**
>
> **Ingredients**
> 6 eggs
>
> **Steps**
> Place the eggs at the bottom of a saucepan.
> Fill the saucepan with enough water to cover the eggs.
> Heat the saucepan on high heat until the water comes to a boil.
> After the water comes to a boil, turn the burner down to medium heat and continue boiling for 8 minutes.
> Strain the water from the pan, and run cold water over the eggs to cool them.
> Peel the eggs under a little running water.
> Serve.

According to the recipe, which action should be completed first?

A) Peel eggs under water.

B) Fill the saucepan with water.

C) Heat the water to a boil.

D) Strain the water from the pan.

16. Babies learn to move their bodies over time. Head control is first developed at two months to create strong neck, back, and tummy muscles. Next, the abilities to reach, grasp, and sit up with support happen around four to six months. By the end of six months, babies learn to roll over. After six to nine months, babies can sit on their own and crawl. During age nine to twelve months, pulling and standing up are mastered. Finally, after gaining good balance, babies take their first steps!

Which BEST describes the order of a baby's movement over time?

A) roll over, control head, sit up, crawl

B) sit up, roll over, crawl, walk

C) control head, reach, crawl, roll over

D) sit up, grasp, crawl, walk

INTERPRETING VERBAL AND GRAPHIC COMMUNICATIONS

Verbal communications can be used to send a message or information to an individual or a group. Memos, advertisements, and flyers are all ways in which ideas and information can be shared. Key elements include the heading, subject, date, message, pictures, and a call to action (information telling readers how to respond).

To better understand what is written, try to identify the author's intention and the purpose of the text. The structure of the text will help clarify the main points. Important parts may be presented in paragraphs, bullet points, or bold print.

Graphic communications are used to locate places, identify parts of an object, and demonstrate processes. Key parts include graphics, labels, numerical data, colors, symbols, and lines that show direction, connections, or relationships among parts.

Table 2.8. Interpreting Verbal and Graphic Communications

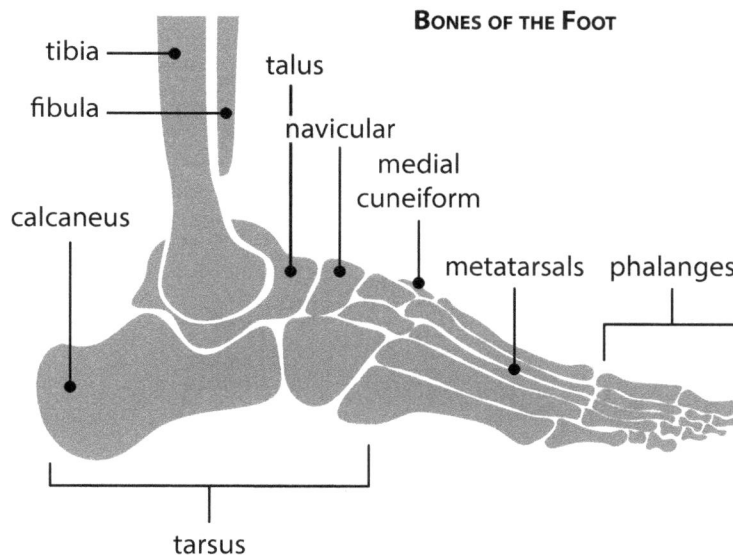

BONES OF THE FOOT

tibia
fibula
talus
navicular
medial cuneiform
calcaneus
metatarsals   phalanges
tarsus

HEADING	Bones of the Foot
PICTURE	visual representation of the parts of the foot
LINES/BRACKETS	outlining sections of the foot
LABELS	providing the name of each part of the foot

17.

> To: All Employees
> From: Dennis Frazier, Manager
> Date: 08/28/17
> Re: Email Communication
>
> This is a reminder of our Email Policy.
> 1. Please refrain from sending company-related emails through personal email accounts. Use company-assigned email accounts for all correspondence.
> 2. Please email managers and team leaders about time off at least three days in advance. Last-minute emails or phone calls are not acceptable.
> 3. Please respond to emails within forty-eight hours, as some are time-sensitive.
>
> Thank you in advance for helping us all work better together!

Which best describes the writer's purpose?

A) to ensure that all employees use email properly

B) to persuade employees to use email more

C) to show appreciation for employees working together

D) to inform all employees of a new email policy

18.

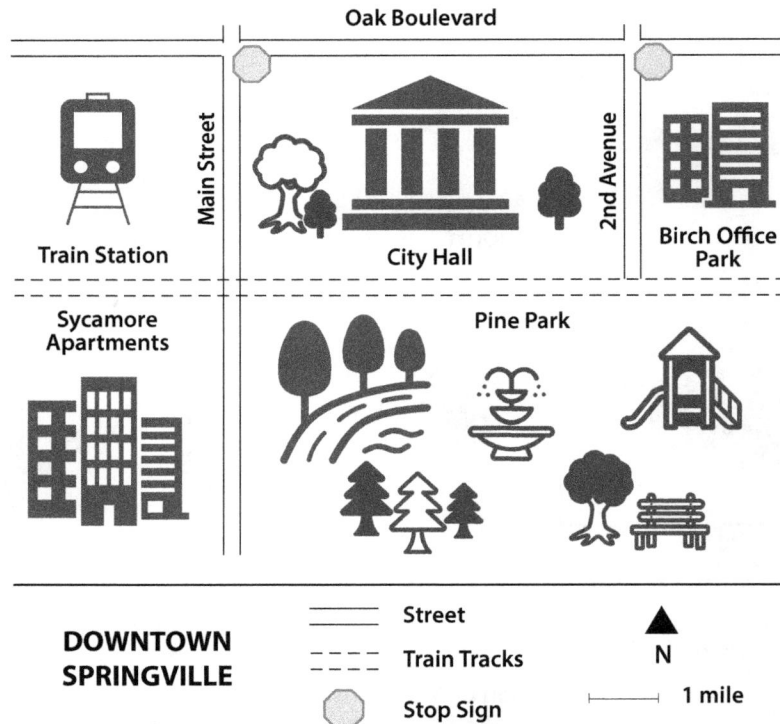

DOWNTOWN SPRINGVILLE

——— Street
- - - - Train Tracks
⬡ Stop Sign

▲
N

⊢——⊣ 1 mile

Jean works at the Birch Office Park and has to go to the train station to go home. If she walks on Oak Boulevard, how many stop signs will she pass?

A) 2

B) 3

C) 4

D) 5

1. **B)** **Correct.** The topic of the passage is geysers. Tourists, volcanic eruptions, and super volcanos are all mentioned in the explanation of what geysers are and how they are formed.

2. **D)** **Correct.** The author writes that "the allied tribes...decisively defeated their US foes," and the remainder of the passage provides details to support this idea.

3. **C)** **Correct.** The passage specifically presents this detail as one of the advantages of subcontracting services.

4. **A)** **Correct.** The statement "It is a great way to advertise their food" is a judgment about how the shops use chalk to show menu items to customers. The word *great* expresses a feeling, and the idea cannot be proven.

5. **D)** **Correct.** After the war, there was a lack of focus on the world and greater focus on personal comforts, which writers viewed as superficiality and materialism.

6. **D)** **Correct.** The text provides details on the experiment as well as its results.

7. **C)** **Correct.** The author states that recycling and reusing objects reduce waste, which helps the environment.

8. **B)** **Correct.** The author demonstrates disapproval of film portrayals of gorillas and how they influence people's views of gorillas.

9. **D)** **Correct.** In this text, two brands of cream are being compared and contrasted.

10. **A)** **Correct.** While phone features are mentioned, the book is about the types of phones listed in the index.

11. **C)** **Correct.** Italics are used to highlight the titles of the books and to emphasize the word *twisted*, which refers to altering a story, not to something being misshapen.

12. **A)** **Correct.** *Fortification* and *fortress* are synonyms. In the seventeenth century, the purpose of the fortress changed. This is a clue that *converted* means "a change in form or function."

13. **A)** **Correct.** The root *cred* means *believe*. The words *evidence*, *reviewed*, and *approved* are context clues hinting that something needs to be believed and accepted.

14. **D)** **Correct.** The author compares the food trucks to "a carnival of delicious treats" using the word *like*.

15. **B)** **Correct.** According to the recipe directions, the saucepan must be filled with water before the other steps listed can occur.

16. **B)** **Correct.** According to the passage, a baby achieves milestones in independent movement in this order. Use the ages and signal words to determine the order of events.

17. **A)** **Correct.** The memo is intended to ensure that all employees are following the same email guidelines. It is a reminder of the existing policy, not a new policy, and includes instructions all employees must follow.

18. **A)** **Correct.** She will pass two stop signs; one at 2nd Avenue and one at Main Street.

3

WRITING

On the Academic Writing section, the IELTS-A asks you to complete two tasks. First, you must review some kind of visual information—an image, a chart, a graph—and describe it in writing. Next, you must write an essay expressing your opinion or perspective on an issue. You will be provided with a prompt and asked to take a position on it.

DESCRIBING VISUAL IMAGES

On the exam, you will encounter a chart, a graph, a diagram, or some similar visual image. You must describe it in approximately 150 words. To accomplish this task, use descriptive language, clarity, and structure. Focus on accurately describing the image, taking into account each detail. Imagine you are explaining it to a person who has never seen such an image before.

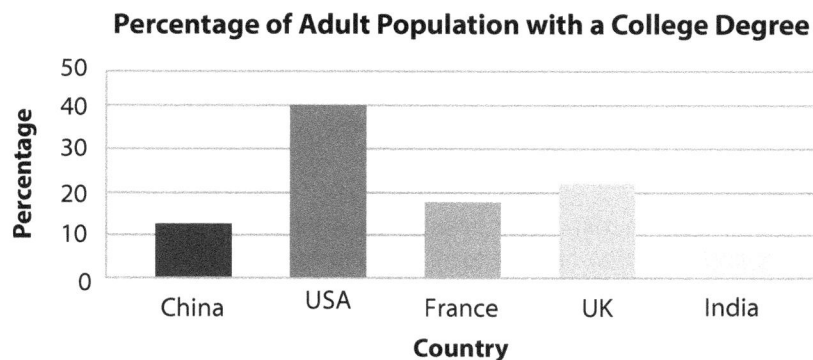

Percentage of Adult Population with a College Degree

Figure 3.1. Graph

The example above (Figure 3.1) contains a bar graph. There are five bars that sit on a horizontal line labelled "Country." A vertical line entitled "Percentage," is marked by five numbers: 10, 20, 30, 40, and 50, reflecting percentages. The five bars represent the populations of college-educated individuals in five countries—China, the United States of

America, France, the United Kingdom, and India. The five bars show how many people in each country are college educated.

The bar representing China is dark colored and solid. It extends just above the 10 on the vertical line, meaning just over 10 percent of people in China are college educated. The bar representing the USA is dark with crossing stripes. It stretches just above 40 on the vertical line, meaning about 40 percent of people in the United States are college educated. The bar representing France is gray with wavy stripes. It extends to about 20 on the vertical line, so about 20 percent of people in France are college educated. The bar representing the UK is light gray with diagonal stripes. It reaches to about 25 on the vertical line, meaning about 25 percent of the people in the United Kingdom are college educated. Finally, the bar representing India is light gray with small circles. It reaches just below 10 on the vertical line, so approximately 9 percent of people in India have a college education.

THE ESSAY

To do well on the essay, you must take a clear side on the issue put forth in the prompt. Support your perspective with strong arguments and specific examples. An effective essay is clearly organized and structured, displays strong vocabulary, and features complex sentences.

> **⚠**
>
> There are two common types of essays. An **expository** essay explains an issue without taking sides or promoting a perspective. A **persuasive** essay argues in favor of or against an issue or perspective. For the IELTS-A, you'll be writing a persuasive essay.

Writing a Thesis Statement

A THESIS STATEMENT articulates the main argument of the essay. No essay is complete without it: the structure and organization of the essay revolve around the thesis statement. The thesis statement is simply the writer's main idea or argument. It usually appears at the end of the introduction.

In a good thesis statement, the author states his or her idea or argument and why it is correct or true.

Example

Take a position on the following topic in your essay. You can choose to write about either of the two viewpoints discussed in the prompt, or you may argue for a third point of view.

Many scientists argue that recent unusual weather patterns, such as powerful hurricanes and droughts, are due to climate change triggered by human activity. They argue that automobiles, oil and gas production, and manufacturing generate carbon emissions that artificially heat the atmosphere, resulting in extreme weather patterns. Others disagree. Some researchers and media pundits argue that climate change is natural, and that extreme weather has always been a feature of Earth's atmosphere.

Possible thesis statements:

- Around the world more people than ever before are driving cars, and industrial production is at an all-time high; it is obvious that human activity is affecting the atmosphere and causing extreme weather events.

- I believe that temperatures and storms are more extreme than ever because of the environmental impact of human activity; not only do scientists have overwhelming evidence that climate change is unnatural, but I can also personally remember when there were fewer storms and variations in temperature.
- Society needs cars and manufacturing, but governments should restrict harmful emissions released into the atmosphere so we can slow down climate change and save lives.

STRUCTURING THE ESSAY

On the IELTS, a strong essay will have an introduction, a body, and a conclusion. While there are many ways to organize an essay, on this exam it is most important that the essay is clearly structured. There is no need to get too complicated: the following simple structure will do.

Introduction

Some writers struggle with the introduction, but it is the best opportunity to present your idea or argument. For the IELTS essay, the introduction can be one paragraph that ends with the thesis statement. In the body of the paragraph, the writer should provide some context for his or her argument. This context might include counterarguments, a preview of specific examples to be discussed later on, acknowledgement of the complexities of the issue, or even a reference to personal experience. The writer can reexamine some of these issues in the conclusion.

> If you're not sure what to include in your introduction, start your essay with just the thesis statement. You can go back and complete the introduction once the rest of the essay is finished.

Example

In the example below, the writer has written an introduction that includes context for her argument: background information, a counterargument, and personal experience. As a result, the reader has a better idea of how complex the issue is and why the writer feels the way she does. The thesis statement appears at the end of the paragraph and, thanks to the introduction as a whole, has more impact.

A century ago, there were barely any cars on the road. Oil had just been discovered in a few parts of the world. Industrial production existed but had not yet exploded with the introduction of the assembly line. Refineries and factories were not yet churning out the chemical emissions they are today. Certainly, hurricanes and droughts occurred, but the populations and infrastructure affected were far smaller. Now, scientists have evidence that human activity—like pollution from industry and cars—is affecting the atmosphere and making weather more extreme. In 2017, millions of people were affected by hurricanes and wildfires. It is true that some researchers disagree that human activity has caused these and other extreme weather events. But why take the risk? If we can limit destruction now and in the future, we should. Extreme weather events are a danger to people all around the world. Society needs cars and manufacturing, but governments should restrict harmful emissions released into the atmosphere so we can slow down climate change and save lives.

The Body Paragraphs

Most writers find the body of the essay the easiest part to write. The body of the essay is simply several paragraphs, each beginning with a topic sentence to address an example that supports the argument made in the thesis statement or, in the case of an expository essay, explains the writer's reasoning. On the IELTS, you may use specific examples, personal anecdotes, present problems and solutions, or compare and contrast ideas. You do not need to refer to any outside literature or documentation.

To strengthen the body of the essay, writers should maintain consistency in paragraphs by always beginning with a topic sentence to introduce the main idea of each paragraph. Each paragraph deals with its own main topic, but writers should use transition words and phrases to link paragraphs with each other. A good essay maintains readability and flow.

Example

This example body paragraph is related to the introduction provided above. It provides reasoning and historical evidence for the author's argument that human activity is negatively impacting the earth and causing climate change.

Human industrial activity has been growing exponentially, putting more pollution into the atmosphere than ever. Over the past forty years, large countries like China and India have become industrialized and manufacture many of the world's products. As their populations become more prosperous, demand for automobiles also rises, putting more cars on the road—and exhaust in the air. While industrial development has benefitted Asia and other areas, carbon emissions that cause climate change have multiplied. Meanwhile, previously industrialized countries in Europe and North America continue to produce carbon emissions. In the nineteenth century, only a few countries had industrial sectors; today, global industry strains the environment like never before. The past 150 years have seen unprecedented industrial growth. Even if the climate changes naturally over time, it cannot be denied that recent human activity has suddenly generated enormous amounts of carbon emissions that have impacted the atmosphere. Scientists say that the earth is warming as a result.

Conclusion

The conclusion does not need to be long. Its purpose is to wrap up the essay, reminding the reader why the topic and the writer's discussion are important. It is an opportunity for the writer to reexamine the thesis statement and ideas posited in the introduction. It is a time to reinforce the argument, not just to repeat the introduction.

Example

This example is taken from the same essay as the introduction and body paragraph above. It reinforces the writer's argument without simply repeating what she said in the introduction. The writer does address the topics she spoke about in the introduction (climate change and protecting people from extreme weather) but she does not simply rewrite the thesis; rather, she calls for action.

No doubt, scientists, pundits, and politicians will continue to argue over the reasons for extreme weather. Meanwhile, Mother Nature will continue to wreak havoc on vulnerable areas regardless of what we think. Because we have proof that climate change is related to extreme weather and we know that extreme weather threatens people's lives, the time to act is now. We can take steps to mitigate pollution without lowering quality of life. Doing anything else is irresponsible—and for some, deadly.

PROVIDING SUPPORTING EVIDENCE

As discussed above, a good essay should have specific evidence or examples that support the thesis statement. On the IELTS, a specific example should be something related to the idea of the paragraph and the essay, not a new idea. A specific example can be from your general knowledge; you do not need to know about specific academic issues to do well on the essay. Remember, you are being tested on your reasoning and argumentative skills.

The following are some examples of general statements and specific statements that provide more detailed support:

GENERAL: Human industrial activity has been growing exponentially, putting more pollution into the atmosphere than ever.

SPECIFIC: Over the past forty years, large countries like China and India have become industrialized and manufacture many of the world's products. As their populations become more prosperous, demand for automobiles also rises, putting more cars on the road—and exhaust in the air.

SPECIFIC: Meanwhile, previously industrialized countries in Europe and North America continue to produce carbon emissions. In the nineteenth century, only a few countries had industrial sectors; today, global industry strains the environment like never before.

GENERAL: More people than ever are affected by extreme weather.

SPECIFIC: In 2017, several hurricanes affected the United States and the Caribbean. In Texas, Hurricane Harvey led to historic flooding in Houston and the Texas Coast. Millions of people were affected; thousands lost their homes, jobs, and livelihoods.

SPECIFIC: Hurricane Irma damaged the US Virgin Islands and neighboring Caribbean nations. Soon after, Hurricane Maria catastrophically devastated Puerto Rico. Months later, Puerto Ricans were still without power and basic necessities. It is still not clear how many have died due to the storm and related damage.

Example

The paragraph below is structured with a topic sentence and specific supporting ideas. This paragraph supports the introduction in the example above.

More people than ever are affected by extreme weather. In 2017, several hurricanes affected the United States and the Caribbean. In Texas, Hurricane Harvey led to historic flooding in Houston and the Texas Coast. Millions of people were affected; thousands lost their homes, jobs, and livelihoods. Hurricane Irma damaged Florida, the US Virgin Islands and neighboring Caribbean nations. Soon after, Hurricane Maria catastrophically devastated Puerto Rico. Months later, Puerto Ricans were still without power and basic necessities. It is still not clear how many have died due to the storm and related damage. In California, severe droughts led to exceptionally large wildfires that threatened Los Angeles and destroyed neighboring communities. Meanwhile, those same areas—Southern California, the Texas Coast, and Florida—continue to grow, putting more people at risk when the next hurricane or fire strikes.

WRITING WELL

Using transitions, complex sentences, and certain words can turn a good description or essay into a great one. Transitions, syntax, word choice, and tone all help clarify and amplify a writer's argument or point and improve the flow of any piece of writing.

Transitions

An essay consists of several paragraphs. TRANSITIONS are words and phrases that help connect the paragraphs and ideas of the text. Most commonly, transitions appear at the beginning of a paragraph, but writers should also use them throughout a text to connect overarching ideas. Common transition words include *also, next, still, although, in addition to*, and *in other words*. A transition shows a relationship between ideas, so writers should pay close attention to the transition words and phrases they choose. Transitions may show connections or contrasts between words and ideas.

Table 3.1. Common Transitions

TRANSITION TYPE	EXAMPLES
addition	additionally, also, as well, further, furthermore, in addition, moreover
cause and effect	as a result, because, consequently, due to, if/then, so, therefore, thus
concluding	briefly, finally, in conclusion, in summary, thus, to conclude
contrast	but, however, in contrast, nevertheless, on the contrary, on the other hand, yet
examples	for example, for instance, in other words
similarity	also, likewise, similarly
time	after, before, currently, later, recently, since, subsequently, then, while

Syntax

SYNTAX refers to how words and phrases are arranged in writing or speech. Writing varied sentences is essential to capturing and keeping a reader's interest. A good essay features different types of sentences: simple, complex, compound, and compound-complex. Sentences need not always begin with the subject; they might start with a transition word or phrase, for instance. Variety is key.

Still, writers should keep in mind that the point of an essay is to convey an idea to the reader, so it is most important that the writing be clear. Clarity should not be sacrificed for the sake of flowery, overly wordy language or confusing syntax.

Word Choice and Tone

Like syntax, WORD CHOICE makes an impression on readers. The IELTS does not test on specific vocabulary or require writers to use specific words on the essay. However, the essay is a good opportunity to use strong vocabulary related to the prompt or issue under discussion. Writers should be careful, though, and have confidence that they understand the words they are using. Writers should also avoid vague, imprecise, or generalizing language like *good, bad, a lot, a little, very, normal*, and so on.

Editing, Revising, and Proofreading

On the IELTS, the writer has a limited amount of time to complete the essay. If there is time for editing or proofreading, writers should hunt for grammar, spelling, or punctuation mistakes that could change the meaning of the text or make it difficult to understand. These include errors such as sentence fragments, run-on sentences, subject-verb disagreement, and pronoun-antecedent disagreement.

4

PRACTICE TEST ONE

LISTENING

Please visit the URL to hear the recordings that accompany the test questions. (You must type this exact address into your browser; the page cannot be accessed from the Trivium website.)
https://www.triviumtestprep.com/ielts-listening

Dialogue One

Directions: Choose the correct letter, A, B, or C.

1. What comes with the standard oil change?
   A) synthetic oil
   B) basic oil
   C) tire rotation

2. Which type of oil only needs changing every 8,000 miles?
   A) basic oil
   B) synthetic oil
   C) natural oil

3. How long does the premium oil change take?
   A) one hour
   B) thirty minutes
   C) twenty minutes

4. The customer needs new
   A) back tires.
   B) front tires.
   C) brakes.

5. What type of oil change is the customer charged for?
   A) standard
   B) premium
   C) deluxe

6. The customer doesn't get the premium oil change because
   A) it is too expensive.
   B) no tire rotation is needed.
   C) it will take too long.

7. How long will the auto service take?
   A) less than twenty minutes
   B) around thirty minutes
   C) more than thirty minutes

8. Basic oil
   A) lasts the longest time.
   B) is the most expensive.
   C) lasts the shortest time.

9. Old tires also cause
   A) oil problems.
   B) rotation.
   C) brake wear.

10. How can the customer pay?
    A) cash
    B) check
    C) credit card

Monologue One

Directions: Label the map below. Choose FIVE answers from the box and write the correct letters A – J next to questions 11 – 20.

LAKE WHITNEY HIGHWAYS

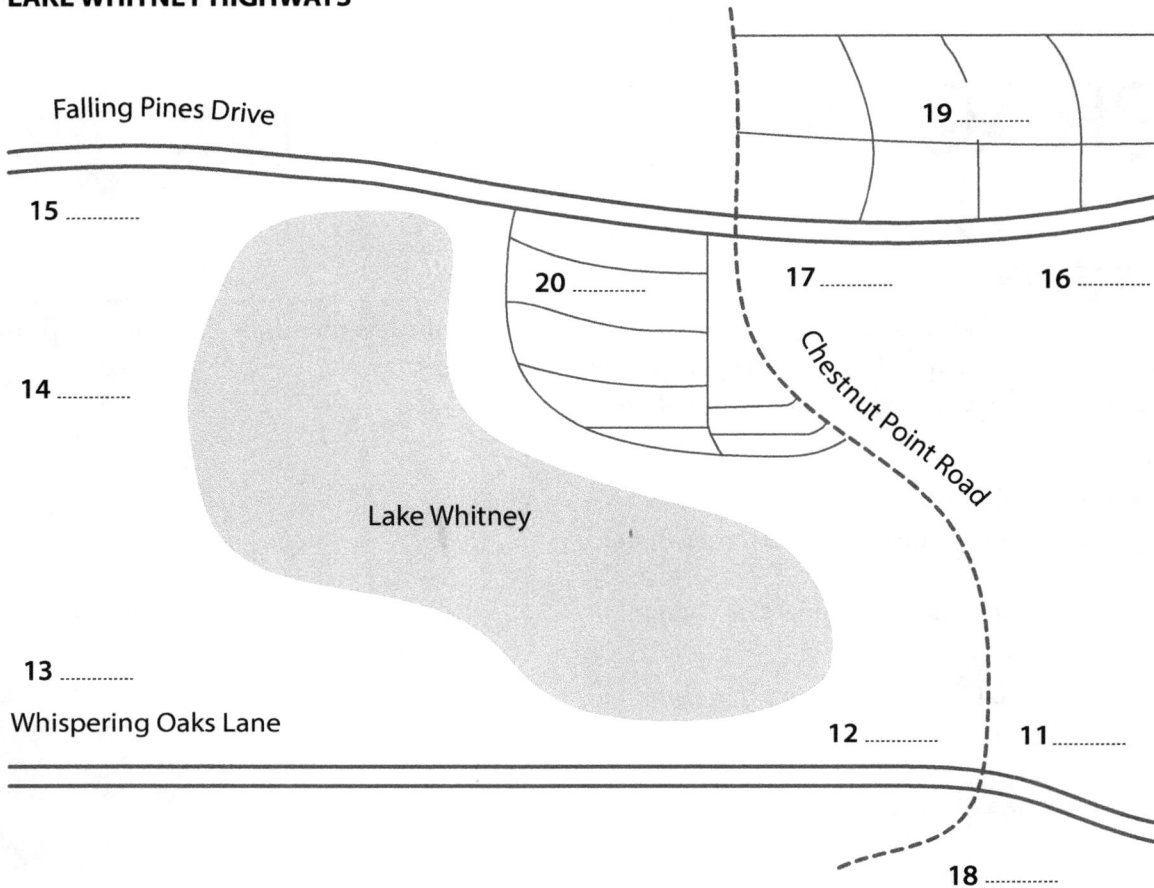

Falling Pines Drive

15 ....

19 ....

20 ....

17 ....

16 ....

14 ....

Lake Whitney

Chestnut Point Road

13 ....

Whispering Oaks Lane

12 ....

11 ....

18 ....

KEY

A—Lake Whitney Chamber of Commerce
B—Lakeside Elementary
C—Loretta's Restaurant
D—J.J.'s Diner
E—Jen's Fitness Studio
F—Sam's Supermarket
G—Hank's Qwik Stop
H—Greg's Yoga
I—Grab 'n' Go + Gas
J—Whitney High School

——— **Residential Street**

- - - - - **Two-Lane Highway**

═══ **Four-Lane Highway**

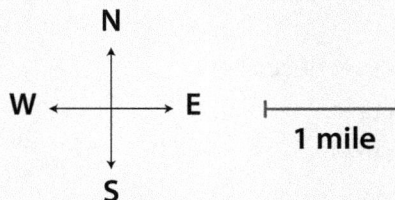

N
W ←→ E
S

├———┤
1 mile

Dialogue Two

Directions: Fill in the blank with the answer from the dialogue. In some cases, more than one word or term may be correct.

21. The weather in Montreal will be_____.

22. Paula is from_____, where it is warm most of the year.

23. The women will go to Montreal within a few_____.

24. Marie has_____, which could let them travel for free.

25. Paula gets out of school early on_____.

26. Marie wants to come back on the 18th because she has_____.

27. If Marie gets back too late on Monday, it will hurt her_____.

28. If the women fly, they can come back on_____.

29. If the women drive, they must come back on_____.

30. Layovers are only fun if they are in a place that is_____.

Monologue Two

Directions: Write no more than three words and/or a number for each answer. In some cases, more than one word or term may be correct.

What two payments need to be made BEFORE moving in?

31. _____

32. _____

What are the TWO different deposit amounts?

33. _____

34. _____

What monthly fees, aside from rent, need to be paid AFTER move-in?

35. _____

36. _____

How can rent be paid, aside from using the mail slot?

37. _____

38. _____

In what TWO ways can rent be paid?

39. _____

40. _____

In its most basic form, geography is the study of space; more specifically, it studies the physical space of the earth and the ways in which it interacts with, shapes, and is shaped by its habitants. Geographers look at the world from a spatial perspective. This means that at the center of all geographic study is the question, "where?" For geographers, the "where" of any interaction, event, or development is a crucial element to understanding it.

This question of "where" can be asked in a variety of fields of study, so there are many sub-disciplines of geography. These can be organized into four main categories: 1) regional studies, which examine the characteristics of a particular place; 2) topical studies, which look at a single physical or human feature that impacts the whole world; 3) physical studies, which focus on the physical features of Earth; and 4) human studies, which examine the relationship between human activity and the environment.

While "*where?*" is the most basic geographic question, it is simply the starting point. To engage in real study, geographers also ask, "*why is it there?*" and "*what are the consequences of it being there?*"

To answer these questions, geographers have developed five themes of geography: Location, Place, Region, Human-Environment Interaction, and Movement. Each of these addresses the basic geographic questions:

LOCATION addresses the question, "*where is it specifically located?*" An example of location would be the address of someone's house or a description of where it is in the neighborhood.

Place and Region both address the question, "*why is it there?*" PLACE asks, "*what is it like there? What are its qualities and characteristics?*" REGION asks, "*what do different areas have in common and why?*"

While the address of a specific house is an example of location, a description of the neighborhood would be an example of *place*. Comparing that neighborhood to others in the area would be an example of *region*.

Human-Environment Interaction and Movement both address the question, "*what are the consequences of it being there?*"

HUMAN-ENVIRONMENT INTERACTION asks, "how do humans shape the environment and how does the environment shape them?" The development of cities illustrates human-environment interaction. For example, San Francisco is known for its steep streets, a result of the physical landscape on which it is built.

Chicago is an example of the human impact on the environment. In 1900, engineers successfully reversed the flow of the river so that it pulled water from Lake Michigan rather than feeding into it.

MOVEMENT asks, "how do places connect to and interact with one another?" Blues music spreading from the South into the rest of the United States and beyond is an example of movement.

All of geography can be organized around these five themes.

Match the topic to the field of study it belongs to.

1.	Regional Studies	
2.	Topical Studies	
3.	Physical Studies	
4.	Human Studies	

- a study of volcanoes and volcanic rock
- a single physical or human feature that impacts the whole world
- research on the impact of agriculture on prairie habitats
- characteristics of a particular place

Match the geographic theme with the question it answers.

5.	Location	
6.	Place	
7.	Region	
8.	Human-Environment Interaction	
9.	Movement	

- How do humans shape the environment and how does the environment shape them?
- How do places connect to and interact with one another?
- Where is it specifically located?
- What is it like there? What are its qualities and characteristics?
- What do different areas have in common and why?

Match the city or region with the example it refers to.

10.	Chicago	
11.	The South	
12.	San Francisco	

- the spread of blues music
- engineers reversing the flow of Lake Michigan
- steep streets

Hand Washing

A

Hand washing is one of the simplest and most powerful ways to fight infection. The idea behind hand washing is simple. Many illnesses are spread when people touch infected surfaces, such as door handles or other people's hands, and then touch their own eyes, mouths, or noses. So, if pathogens can be removed from the hands before they spread, infections can be prevented. When done correctly, hand washing can prevent the spread of many dangerous bacteria and viruses, including those that cause the flu, the common cold, diarrhea, and many acute respiratory illnesses.

B

Basically, hand washing requires only soap and water. Just twenty seconds of scrubbing with soap and a complete rinsing with water is enough to kill and/or wash away many pathogens. The process doesn't even require warm water—studies have shown that cold water is just as effective at reducing the number of microbes on the hands. Antibacterial soaps are also available, although several studies have shown that simple soap and cold water is just as effective.

C

In recent years, hand sanitizers have become popular as an alternative to hand washing. These gels, liquids, and foams contain a high concentration of alcohol (usually at least 60 percent) that kills most bacteria and fungi; they can also be effective against some, but not all, viruses. There is a downside to hand sanitizer, however. Because the sanitizer isn't rinsed from hands, it only kills pathogens and does nothing to remove organic matter. So, hands "cleaned" with hand sanitizer may still harbor pathogens. Thus, while hand sanitizer can be helpful in situations where soap and clean water isn't available, a simple hand washing is still the best option.

Glossary

bacteria: tiny life form that can cause sickness or disease

pathogen: bacteria or virus that can cause disease

microbes: bacteria that can cause disease

hand sanitizers: gels, foams, or liquids that clean hands without water

downside: problem

Answer the following questions based on the information provided in the article.

13. What is the purpose of hand washing?

14. Why do illnesses spread when people touch infected surfaces?

15. Is hand washing complicated or simple?

16. What diseases can hand washing help prevent?

17. Hand washing only requires what two substances?

18. How long do you need to scrub to kill pathogens?

19. Is warm water necessary to reduce microbes?

20. When did hand sanitizers become popular?

21. What product does hand sanitizer contain that kills bacteria and fungi?

22. What is the downside to hand sanitizer?

This article has three paragraphs: A, B, and C. Below are suggested headings for each paragraph. Match the heading to the paragraph it best describes.

23. Paragraph A	
24. Paragraph B	
25. Paragraph C	

- The Process of Hand Washing
- Fighting Infection with Hand Washing
- Hand Sanitizers: An Alternative to Hand Washing?

The Solar System and Beyond is Awash with Water

The following passage and table are adapted from an article entitled "The Solar System and Beyond Is Awash with Water," published online by the National Aeronautics and Space Administration (NASA) in April 2015.

As NASA missions explore our solar system and search for new worlds, they are finding water in surprising places. Water is but one piece of our search for habitable planets and life beyond Earth, yet it links many seemingly unrelated worlds in surprising ways.

"NASA science activities have provided a wave of amazing findings related to water in recent years that inspire us to continue investigating our origins and the fascinating possibilities for other worlds, and life, in the universe," said Ellen Stofan, chief scientist for the agency. "In our lifetime, we may very well finally answer whether we are alone in the solar system and beyond."

The chemical elements in water, hydrogen and oxygen, are some of the most abundant elements in the universe. Astronomers see the signature of water in giant molecular clouds between the stars, in disks of material that represent newborn planetary systems, and in the atmospheres of giant planets orbiting other stars.

There are several worlds thought to possess liquid water beneath their surfaces, and many more that have water in the form of ice or vapor. Water is found in primitive bodies like comets and asteroids, and dwarf planets like Ceres. The atmospheres and interiors of the four giant planets—Jupiter, Saturn, Uranus, and Neptune—are thought to contain enormous quantities of the wet stuff, and their moons and rings have substantial water ice.

Perhaps the most surprising water worlds are the five icy moons of Jupiter and Saturn that show strong evidence of oceans beneath their surfaces: Ganymede, Europa, and Callisto at Jupiter, and Enceladus and Titan at Saturn.

Scientists using NASA's Hubble Space Telescope recently provided powerful evidence that Ganymede has a saltwater, sub-surface ocean, likely sandwiched between two layers of ice.

Europa and Enceladus are thought to have an ocean of liquid water beneath their surface in contact with mineral-rich rock, and may have the three ingredients needed for life as we know it: liquid water, essential chemical elements for biological processes, and sources of energy that could be used by living things.

Understanding the distribution of water in our solar system tells us a great deal about how the planets, moons, comets, and other bodies formed 4.5 billion years ago from the disk of gas and dust that surrounded our sun. The space closer to the sun was hotter and drier than the space farther from the sun, which was cold enough for water to condense. The dividing line, called the "frost line," sat around Jupiter's present-day orbit. Even today, this is the approximate distance from the sun at which the ice on most comets begins to melt and become "active." Their brilliant spray releases water ice, vapor, dust, and other chemicals, which are thought to form the bedrock of most worlds of the frigid outer solar system.

Scientists think it was too hot in the solar system's early days for water to condense into liquid or ice on the inner planets, so it had to be delivered—possibly by comets and water-bearing asteroids. NASA's Dawn mission is currently studying Ceres, which is the largest body in the asteroid belt between Mars and Jupiter. Researchers think Ceres might have a water-rich composition similar to some of the bodies that brought water to the three rocky, inner planets, including Earth.

The amount of water in the giant planet Jupiter holds a critical missing piece to the puzzle of our solar system's formation. Jupiter was likely the first planet to form, and it contains most of the material that wasn't incorporated into the sun. The leading theories about its formation rest on the amount of water the planet soaked up.

It's easy to forget that the story of Earth's water, from gentle rains to raging rivers, is intimately connected to the larger story of our solar system and beyond. But our water came from somewhere—every world in our solar system got its water from the same shared source. So it's worth considering that the next glass of water you drink could easily have been part of a comet, or an ocean moon, or a long-vanished sea on the surface of Mars. And note that the night sky may be full of exoplanets formed by similar processes to our home world, where gentle waves wash against the shores of alien seas.

Moons of Jupiter and Saturn

NAME (DESCRIPTION)	DISTANCE FROM SUN (IN ASTRONOMICAL UNITS)	OCEAN WORLD STATUS
Europa (moon of Jupiter)	5.2 AU	Active
Ganymede (moon of Jupiter)	5.2 AU	Locked (under ice)
Callisto (moon of Jupiter)	5.2 AU	Locked (under ice)
Enceladus (moon of Saturn)	9.5 AU	Active
Titan (moon of Saturn)	9.5 AU	Locked (under ice)

Glossary

solar system: the sun and planets in our region of outer space

abundant: common

vapor: water in gas form; fog

comet: a celestial body made up of ice and dust, that develops a tail, with an irregular orbit

asteroid: a small, rocky celestial body

asteroid belt: a region of interplanetary space between Mars and Jupiter where many asteroids exist

Do the following statements agree with the information given in the text?

For questions 26 – 32, write:

- TRUE if the statement agrees with the information
- FALSE if the statement contradicts the information
- UNCERTAIN if there is no information on this

26. NASA explorers are finding water in surprising places.
27. Hydrogen and oxygen are some of the most common elements in the universe.
28. Water is only known to be found on planet Earth.
29. Scientists believe that the moon Ganymede has a saltwater, sub-surface ocean.
30. The moons Europa and Enceladus contain three ingredients needed for life: liquid water, essential chemical elements, and sources of energy that could be used by living things.

31. Jupiter was likely the first planet to form.

32. Water on Earth is not connected to water found on any other planets.

Answer the following questions based on the information provided in the article.

33. The chemical elements in water are _____.

34. The three moons of Jupiter that show evidence of oceans beneath their surfaces are _____, _____, and _____.

35. The two moons of Saturn that show evidence of oceans beneath their surfaces are _____ and _____.

36. What is the "frost line"?

37. Scientists think water was delivered to the inner planets of the solar system by _____ and _____.

38. Jupiter contains most of the material _____.

Questions 39 and 40 refer to the table entitled "Moons of Jupiter and Saturn."

39. Which moon of Jupiter has an "Active" ocean world status?

40. Which moon of Saturn has an "Active" ocean world status?

WRITING

Writing Task One

You should spend about twenty minutes on this task.

The bar graph compares the number of scoops of ice cream consumed by four children at school lunch over a three-week period.

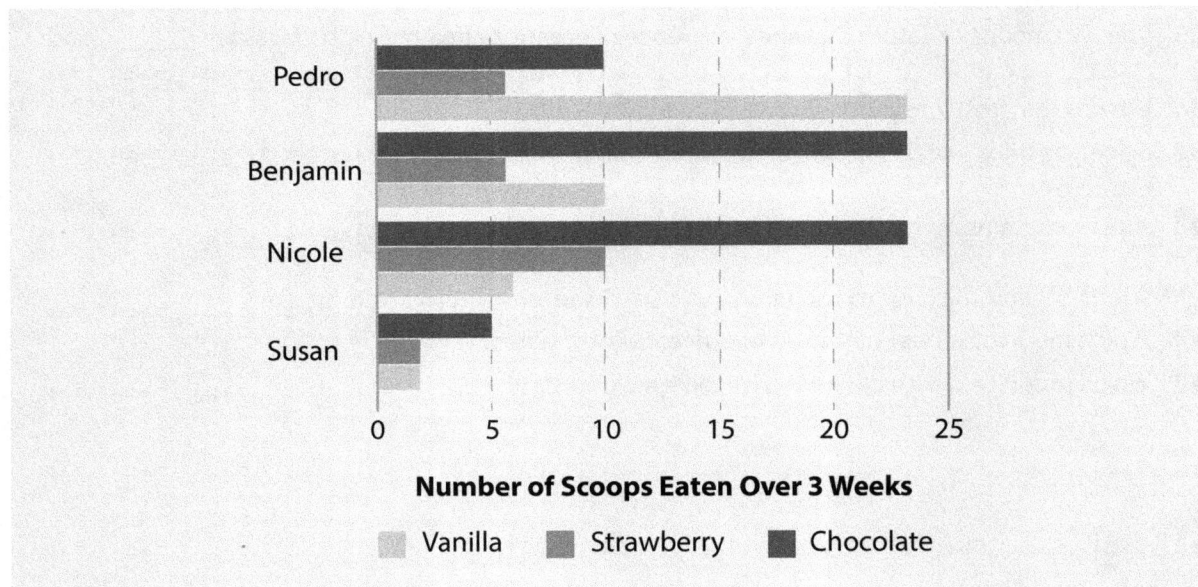

Number of Scoops Eaten Over 3 Weeks

Vanilla ■ Strawberry ■ Chocolate

Summarize the information by selecting and reporting the main features and making comparisons where relevant. Write at least 150 words.

Writing Task Two

You should spend about 40 minutes on this task.

Write about the following topic:

> The rise in popularity of e-cigarettes has reduced the overall smoking rate according to government health agencies. Many people believe the new technology has helped smokers quit traditional tobacco cigarettes. However, others raise concerns about the appeal of e-cigarettes to young people and advocate government regulation of e-cigarettes to prevent negative side effects of their use on a new generation of smokers.
>
> Should e-cigarettes be regulated by the government?

In your essay, take a position on this question. Give reasons for your answer and include any relevant examples from your own knowledge or experience. Write at least 250 words.

ANSWER KEY

LISTENING

Dialogue One

A customer is talking to a mechanic about auto services; this is part of the conversation.

A: We have three types of oil changes: the standard, the deluxe, and the premium. With the standard, you get an oil change with basic oil and a vehicle check. With the deluxe, you get an oil change with synthetic oil and a vehicle check. With the premium, you get synthetic oil, a vehicle check, and a tire rotation.

B: Sorry, what is the difference between basic oil and synthetic oil?

A: With basic oil, you need an oil change every 3,000 miles. With synthetic oil, you can go up to 8,000 miles.

B: Which one can be done in the shortest time?

A: The standard and deluxe both take about twenty minutes. How long do you have?

B: I only have about thirty minutes. Can the premium be done in that time?

A: Yes.

B: OK. I don't think the tire rotation really matters though.

A: It depends on how new your tires are. If your tires are pretty new, then you're probably OK. If your tires are old, the brakes may also wear.

B: Both my front tires are new. I need to get back tires soon.

A: We could probably replace them just as easily as we could rotate them. I could do that for about $200, and I could get you out of here in half an hour or less.

B: OK. Give me the synthetic oil change and the new tires.

A: I will just charge you for the deluxe oil change and the tires then. The total will be $250 plus tax.

B: Do you take credit cards?

A: No, cash only.

ANSWERS

1. **B) is correct.** Only the premium oil change comes with a tire rotation. Speaker A says, "With the standard, you get an oil change with basic oil and a vehicle check."

2. **B) is correct.** Speaker A says, "With synthetic oil, you can go up to 8,000 miles."

3. **B) is correct.** Speaker B says, "I only have about thirty minutes. Can the premium be done in that time?" Speaker A responds, "Yes."

4. **A) is correct.** Speaker B, the customer, says "I need to get back tires soon."

5. **C) is correct.** The customer is charged for the deluxe oil change and the tire rotation. At the end of the dialogue, Speaker A says,

"I will just charge you for the deluxe oil change and the tires then."

6. **B) is correct.** The customer says that she needs new tires, not a tire rotation.

7. **B) is correct.** The mechanic tells the customer that "I could get you out of here in half an hour or less."

8. **C) is correct.** The mechanic says, "With basic oil, you need an oil change every 3,000 miles. With synthetic oil, you can go up to 8,000 miles."

9. **C) is correct.** Speaker A says, "If your tires are old, the brakes may also wear."

10. **A) is correct.** Speaker B asks, "Do you take credit cards?" Speaker A responds, "No, cash only."

Monologue One

The president of the Lake Whitney Chamber of Commerce is speaking to a group of people about where various businesses are located.

Some of our town's most important businesses are located in the area immediately surrounding Lake Whitney. The first business I want to talk about is the building we are in now, the Lake Whitney Chamber of Commerce. We are located on Whispering Oaks Lane, just east of Chestnut Point Road. Two other very active businesses are also located on Whispering Oaks Lane: Loretta's Restaurant on the Lake, just south of the lake, and JJ's Diner, located at the far west end of town. Of course, it's not as far west as Sam's Supermarket. It's kind of in the middle of nowhere, not even on a major road! Falling Pines Drive is the other four-lane highway in town, and it is home to two schools: Lakeside Elementary School, which is just north of the lake, and Whitney High School, which is at the far east end of Falling Pines Drive. The community has two gas stations, both located on Chestnut Point Road: Hank's Qwik Stop, located near the intersection of Chestnut Point Road and Falling Pines Drive, and Grab n' Go + Gas, located at the far south end of Chestnut Point Road. There are also two businesses that make their homes in residential communities: Jen's Fitness Studio, located just north of Falling Pines Drive, and Greg's Yoga, which is located just south of Falling Pines Drive, near the lake.

LAKE WHITNEY HIGHWAYS

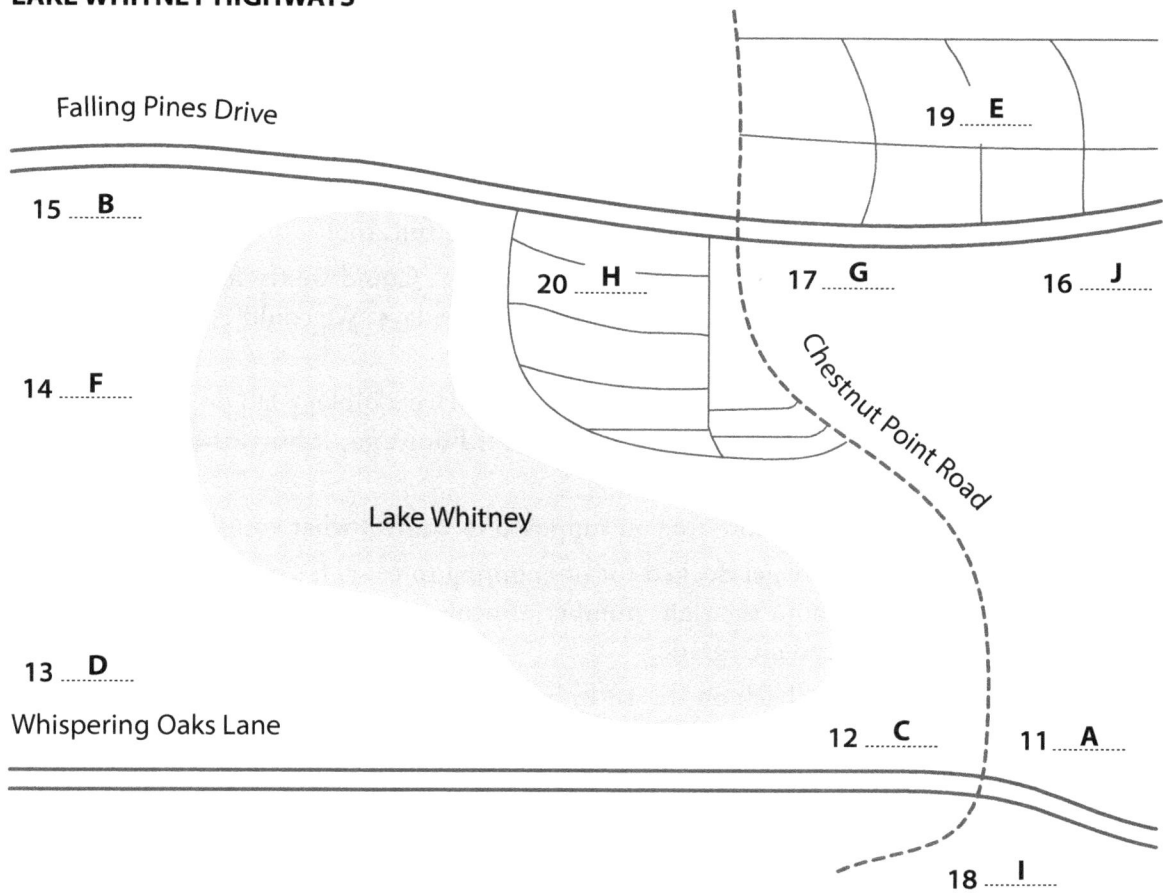

Falling Pines Drive

15 **B**

19 **E**

20 **H**

17 **G**

16 **J**

14 **F**

Chestnut Point Road

Lake Whitney

13 **D**

Whispering Oaks Lane

12 **C**

11 **A**

18 **I**

KEY

A—Lake Whitney Chamber of Commerce
B—Lakeside Elementary
C—Loretta's Restaurant
D—J.J.'s Diner
E—Jen's Fitness Studio
F—Sam's Supermarket
G—Hank's Qwik Stop
H—Greg's Yoga
I—Grab 'n' Go + Gas
J—Whitney High School

——— Residential Street

- - - - - Two-Lane Highway

═══ Four-Lane Highway

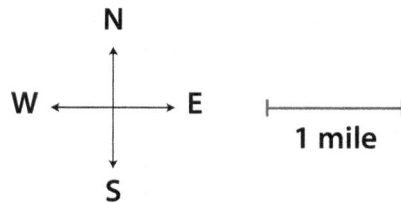

1 mile

Dialogue Two

Two friends are making travel plans.

Paula: Montreal would be a great weekend trip. I think it's cold there in the fall, though. We'd have to wear sweaters.

Marie: No big deal. I have tons of sweaters! I'm from Minnesota where it's cold all the time. I have some sweaters and coats you can borrow if you need to. I know it doesn't get very cold in Florida.

Paula: Thanks! When would you want to go? Like, soon?

Marie: Maybe within a few weeks, yes. We could drive up. It is only a six-hour drive. Or we could fly. I have a voucher for two free flights. Of course, it will probably only work on flights with a layover. But those can be kind of fun, too!

Paula: Only if the layover is in some interesting place. . . . Could we try for the weekend of the 17th and 18th? I get out of class at 1:15 on Fridays. We could even leave on the 16th maybe.

Marie: We'd have to come back on the 18th, though. I have a biology lab on Monday that I can't miss. We get graded on attendance, and if I don't go, it hurts the grades of my lab partners also.

Paula: That doesn't seem fair! How are you supposed to control what your lab partners do?

Marie: Well, it's not that they get docked for not coming to class. It's just that the labs are very hard to do without the right number of people. I'd be letting them down, and it would hurt my attendance grade.

Paula: I'm fine with coming back on the 18th, but later in the day. Or . . . what time is your biology lab?

Marie: Three o'clock.

Paula: If we fly, we could come back early on Monday, and you'd still make it to your lab. If we drive, we'd probably have to come back on Sunday.

ANSWERS

21. cold

Paula says, "Montreal would be a great weekend trip. I think it's cold there in the fall, though."

22. Florida

Marie says, "I have some sweaters and coats you can borrow if you need to. I know it doesn't get very cold in Florida."

23. weeks

Marie says, "Maybe within a few weeks, yes."

24. vouchers/free flights/plane tickets

Marie says, "I have a voucher for two free flights."

25. Fridays

Paula says, "I get out of class at 1:15 on Fridays."

26. biology lab/class/biology

Marie says, "We'd have to come back on the 18th, though. I have a biology lab on Monday that I can't miss."

27. attendance grade/grade/lab partners

Marie says, "I'd be letting them down, and it would hurt my attendance grade."

28. Monday

Paula says, "If we fly, we could come back early on Monday, and you'd still make it to your lab."

29. Sunday

Paula says, "If we drive, we'd probably have to come back on Sunday."

30. interesting

Paula says, "Only if the layover is in some interesting place."

Monologue Two

Hi, everyone. I'm Tina, and I'll be speaking with you today about living at Harbor Village Student Apartments. It is important to know a few things before you move in so that you can focus on school and not have to worry if you are forgetting something pertaining to your housing.

Before we issue your set of apartment keys, you will need to pay the deposit and first month's rent. The deposit is five hundred dollars for no pets and eight hundred dollars if you have a pet, such as a cat or dog under ten pounds. You can pay these fees with either a money order or wire transfer.

Once you move in, you will be responsible for the monthly rent, electric bill, and water bill. The rent is due the first of every month—even if the first is on a weekend—and can be paid by check or money order. You can drop the rent in the mail slot in front of the leasing office, pay in person, or set up auto payment. There is a one-hundred-dollar fee for any returned checks. I suggest you open a bank account and set up auto payment as soon as possible; this way, you will not have to worry about remembering to pay rent or late payments.

You will need to pay the electric and water bills directly to each company. The electric and water companies also use an auto-payment option, and the staff here will be happy to help you set that up.

Answers

31. deposit

32. first month's rent

Tina says, "Before we issue your set of apartment keys, you will need to pay the deposit and first month's rent."

33. $500

34. $800

Tina says, "The deposit is five hundred dollars for no pets and eight hundred dollars if you have a pet, such as a cat or dog under ten pounds."

35. electric bill

36. water bill

Tina says, "Once you move in, you will be responsible for the monthly rent, electric bill, and water bill."

37. in person

38. auto payment

Tina says, "You can drop the rent in the mail slot in front of the leasing office, pay in person, or set up auto payment."

39. check

40. money order

Tina says, "rent ...can be paid by check or money order."

1. Regional Studies: characteristics of a particular place

2. Topical Studies: a single physical or human feature that impacts the whole world

3. Physical Studies: a study of volcanoes and volcanic rock

4. Human Studies: research on the impact of agriculture on prairie habitats

5. Location: Where is it specifically located?

6. Place: What is it like there? What are its qualities and characteristics?

7. Region: What do different areas have in common and why?

8. Human-Environment Interaction: How do humans shape the environment and how does the environment shape them?

9. Movement: How do places connect to and interact with one another?

10. Chicago: engineers reversing the flow of Lake Michigan

11. The South: the spread of blues music

12. San Francisco: steep streets

13. to fight infection

14. because people touch their own eyes, mouths, or noses

15. simple

16. the flu, the common cold, diarrhea, and many acute respiratory illnesses

17. soap and water

18. 20 seconds

19. no

20. in recent years

21. alcohol

22. It only kills pathogens and does not remove organic matter.

23. Paragraph A: Fighting Infection with Hand Washing

24. Paragraph B: The Process of Hand Washing

25. Paragraph C: Hand Sanitizers: An Alternative to Hand Washing?

26. **True.** The article states, "As NASA missions explore our solar system and search for new worlds, they are finding water in surprising places."

27. **True.** The article states, "The chemical elements in water, hydrogen and oxygen, are some of the most abundant elements in the universe."

28. **False.** According to the article, "There are several worlds thought to possess liquid water beneath their surfaces, and many more that have water in the form of ice or vapor." The text goes on to name comets, asteroids, and some planets and dwarf planets suspected or known to contain water, vapor, or ice.

29. **True.** The text states that researchers "using NASA's Hubble Space Telescope recently provided powerful evidence that Ganymede has a saltwater, sub-surface ocean, likely sandwiched between two layers of ice."

30. **Uncertain.** It is not clear if Europa and Enceladus contain the three ingredients

for life. The text only states that "Europa and Enceladus are thought to have an ocean of liquid water beneath their surface in contact with mineral-rich rock, and may have the three ingredients needed for life as we know it: liquid water, essential chemical elements for biological processes, and sources of energy that could be used by living things."

31. **True.** According to the text, "Jupiter was likely the first planet to form, and it contains most of the material that wasn't incorporated into the sun."

32. **False.** In the last paragraph, the article says, "our water came from somewhere— every world in our solar system got its water from the same shared source."

33. hydrogen and oxygen

34. Ganymede, Europa, and Callisto

35. Enceladus and Titan

36. the approximate distance from the sun at which the ice on most comets begins to melt and become "active"

37. comets and water-bearing asteroids

38. that wasn't incorporated into the sun

39. Europa. According to the table, Europa is the only moon of Jupiter with an "Active" ocean world status.

40. Enceladus. According to the table, Enceladus is the only moon of Saturn with an "Active" ocean world status.

WRITING

Writing Task One

This bar graph illustrates the amounts of different flavors of ice cream (vanilla, strawberry, and chocolate) consumed by four students over a three-week period. Units are measured in scoops. The four students (Pedro, Benjamin, Nicole, and Susan) ate all three types of ice cream over the three-week period. However, they each ate varying amounts of each flavor.

Susan, who ate the least amount of ice cream overall, ate the most scoops of chocolate at five scoops. She ate only two scoops of vanilla and strawberry.

Like Susan, Nicole and Benjamin also ate more scoops of chocolate ice cream as compared to the other two flavors. Nicole and Benjamin both ate around twenty-three scoops of chocolate ice cream! This is more than double the amount eaten by the other two children. Nicole ate ten scoops of strawberry ice cream and six scoops of vanilla ice cream. Benjamin, unlike Nicole, ate more vanilla than strawberry. He ate ten scoops of vanilla and only six scoops of strawberry over the three-week period.

Unlike the other three children, who ate more chocolate ice cream than any other flavor, Pedro ate the most scoops of vanilla ice cream at twenty-three scoops over the three-week period. His second choice was chocolate, and he ate ten scoops of this flavor. He ate only six scoops of strawberry ice cream.

Writing Task Two

The number of youth smoking traditional cigarettes has never been lower. But electronic cigarettes (e-cigarettes) have skyrocketed in popularity. E-cigarettes should be regulated by the government to prevent youth from smoking since the long-term effects of e-cig use are unknown, youth are still becoming addicted to nicotine, and e-cigs could be a gateway to traditional smoking.

Smoking has long been a way for young people to feel cool or sophisticated. Although traditional smoking is no longer considered cool, the use of e-cigarettes, or vaping, is more and more widely accepted. E-cigarettes are not regulated by the government, so there are no restrictions on their advertisement. This allows e-cig companies to reach youth through a wide range of media. Furthermore, the design of e-cigs and the variety of flavors make them especially appealing to youth.

This is particularly concerning as the long-term effects of vaping are not yet known. The technology is too new to have been studied adequately. The government must study a drug for years before it can become available to the general public. Yet this device that delivers a highly addictive substance is unregulated. It may be true that e-cigarettes are healthier for smokers than traditional cigarettes, but we still do not know the impact on young people.

In addition, we do know that nicotine is a highly addictive drug. Nicotine use could alter the brain chemistry of young people. Even if vaping does not become a gateway to hard drug use, it does make the leap to traditional smoking much more likely.

The government has a responsibility to protect the public's health: regulation is needed to protect young people and help a generation live longer, healthier lives.

PRACTICE TEST TWO

LISTENING

Please visit the URL to hear the recordings that accompany the test questions. (You must type this exact address into your browser; the page cannot be accessed from the Trivium website.)
https://www.triviumtestprep.com/ielts-listening

Dialogue One

Directions: Write no more than three words and/or a number for each answer. In some cases, more than one word or term may be correct.

Mae goes to study groups on which TWO days?

1._____

2._____

In what TWO ways do the study groups help Mae?

3._____

4._____

Raul goes to study groups on which TWO days?

5._____

6._____

Which study groups are run by a TA?

7._____

8._____

At what TWO times does the Monday night study group meet?

9._____

10._____

Monologue One

Directions: Choose the correct letter, A, B, or C.

11. When are you NOT required to take a sixty-hour driver training course?
    A) you have no driver's license at all
    B) you have a driver's license from a reciprocal country
    C) you think you already know how to drive in the US

12. What is Regina Cantor's job?

   A) director of education

   B) head driving instructor

   C) vice president

13. What does the sixty-hour training course cover?

   A) how to get a driver's license in Texas

   B) who is a qualified, licensed driver

   C) rules of the road and safety laws

14. The $350 driver training course includes

   A) the cost for a permit.

   B) two hours of road training.

   C) four hours of road training.

15. If a person already has a driver's license from another country with a reciprocal relationship with the US, then the person must

   A) pass a written test.

   B) pass a driving test.

   C) take a training course.

16. A permit allows a driver to

   A) drive on most roads.

   B) drive on highways only.

   C) drive with a qualified driver.

17. The period in which a driver has a permit is called a

   A) classroom period.

   B) road training period.

   C) probationary period.

18. Where will Hillside Driving Academy help students get a driver's license?

   A) Texas

   B) their home country

   C) any state in the US

19. You can take driver training classes either in a classroom or

   A) by mail.

   B) online.

   C) by phone.

20. What will Regina Cantor do next?

   A) take everyone on a tour

   B) take everyone's registration

   C) begin teaching the class

Dialogue Two

Directions: Write the correct letter A, B, or C next to questions 21 – 27. You may choose any letter more than once.

> Will Gavin take the following classes?
> **A)** Gavin will likely take the class.
> **B)** Gavin likely won't take the class.
> **C)** Gavin may or may not take the class.

21. English Romantic Poets

22. classes in literary criticism

23. Basic Rhetoric and Composition

24. Creative Writing

25. Shakespearean Media

26. Medieval Vision Literature

27. Chaucer's Life and Literature

Directions: Write the correct letter A, B, or C next to questions 28 – 30. You may choose any letter more than once.

> Who teaches the class?
> **A)** Dr. Peters teaches the class.
> **B)** Dr. Summers teaches the class.
> **C)** Leila doesn't know who teaches it.

28. Medieval Vision Literature

29. Chaucer's Life and Literature

30. Rhetoric and Composition

Monologue Two

Directions: Write the correct letter—A, B, or C—next to questions 31 – 40. You may choose any letter more than once.

> **A** — a good idea
> **B** — may or may not be a good idea
> **C** — a bad idea

31. getting a job or internship in the first year of college

32. getting a full-time job or internship

33. getting an unpaid internship

34. working less than 10 hours per week

35. choosing a job based on its fit

36. taking a job because your friends work there

37. working for friends or family

38. dog or house sitting as a job

39. working late hours

40. telling your employer you are a student

A

Providing adequate nutrition is one of the most important responsibilities of acute and long-term care facilities. Patients enter these facilities with a wide range of health issues from fractures and infections to dementia or cancer. Because the needs of every patient are different, it's the task of every health care facility to ensure that patients receive the proper nutrition.

B

Patients, like all people, have two basic nutritional needs: they require macronutrients, the carbohydrates, fats, and proteins that provide energy; and micronutrients, which are the vitamins and elements the body needs to function properly. A good diet will provide the appropriate amount of macronutrients, or calories, to keep the patients energized and full without leading to weight gain, while also providing necessary amounts of micronutrients. Such a diet will help patients remain comfortable and heal properly. A poor diet, on the other hand, can make recovery significantly more difficult.

C

The energy needs of patients can vary widely. Generally, energy needs are directly related to a person's weight and inversely related to age; it's also generally true that men require more calories than women. Thus, a thirty-five-year-old woman who weighs 135 pounds will require around 1800 calories a day, while an older woman would require fewer calories, and a heavier woman would require more. A man of the same age and weight would require 2000 calories a day.

D

Activity level also has a significant impact on a patient's energy needs. A bedridden patient will obviously expend fewer calories and thus will need to eat fewer calories. An elderly, bedridden woman can need as little as 8.5 calories per pound of body weight: if such a patient weighed 135 pounds, she would need only 1150 calories a day. However, many patients, bedridden or otherwise, have hidden energy needs. The process of healing can be extremely energy intensive— even an immobile patient can use up vast reserves of calories as her body fights infection, knits a fracture, or heals bed sores. Patients on a low-energy diet may also develop deficiencies in micronutrients if the quality of their meals is not monitored closely.

Which paragraph contains the following information?

1. the energy needs of a thirty-five-year-old woman who weighs 135 pounds
2. the definition of a micronutrient
3. how many calories an elderly, bedridden woman might need per pound of body weight
4. the definition of a macronutrient
5. whether the process of healing requires a lot of energy

Answer the following questions based on the information provided in the article.

6. One of the most important responsibilities of acute and long-term care facilities is to provide _____.
7. The needs of every patient are _____.
8. The two basic nutritional needs all people have are _____ and _____.
9. Macronutrients are the _____, _____, and _____ that provide energy.

10. Micronutrients are the _____ and _____ the body needs to function properly.

11. Generally, men require _____ calories than women.

12. A thirty-five-year-old woman who weighs 135 pounds needs about _____ calories a day.

13. A thirty-five-year-old man who weighs 135 pounds needs about _____ calories a day.

14. An elderly, bedridden woman who weighs 135 pounds needs about _____ calories a day.

Do the following statements agree with the information given in the text?

For questions 15 – 16 on your answer sheet, write:

- TRUE if the statement agrees with the information
- FALSE if the statement contradicts the information
- UNCERTAIN if there is no information on this

15. Healing can require a lot of energy.

16. Patients on a low-energy diet may become deficient in micronutrients.

This article has three paragraphs, A, B, C, and D. Below are suggested headings for each paragraph. Match the heading to the paragraph it best describes.

- *Different Patients Have Different Needs*
- *Micro Versus Macro: The Basics of Nutrition*
- *Hidden Energy Needs Make a Difference*
- *Patient Nutrition and Facility Responsibility*

17. Paragraph A	
18. Paragraph B	
19. Paragraph C	
20. Paragraph D	

Credit Scores

Credit scores, which range from 300 to 850, are a single value that summarizes an individual's credit history. Pay your bills late? Your credit score will be lower than someone who gets that electric bill filed on the first of every month. Just paid off your massive student loans? You can expect your credit score to shoot up. The companies that manage credit scores actually keep track of all the loans, credit cards, and bill payments in your name. This massive amount of information is summed up in a credit report, which is then reported in a single value: your credit score.

Credit scores are used by many institutions that need to evaluate the risk of providing loans, rentals, or services to individuals. Banks use credit scores when deciding whether to hand out loans; they can also use them to determine the terms of the loan itself. Similarly, car dealers, landlords, and credit card companies will likely all access your credit report before agreeing to do business with you. Even your employer can access a modified version of your credit report (although it will not have your actual credit score on it).

When it comes to credit, everyone begins with a clean slate. The first time you access any credit—be it a credit card, student loan, or rental agreement—information begins to accumulate in your credit report. Thus, having no credit score can often be just as bad as having a low one. Lenders want to know that you have a history of borrowing money and paying it back on time.

After all, if you've never taken out a loan, how can a bank know that you'll pay back its money? So, having nothing on your credit report can result in low credit limits and high interest rates.

With time, though, credit scores can be raised. With every payment, your credit report improves and banks will be more likely to loan you money. These new loans will in turn raise your score even further (as long as you keep making payments, of course).

In general, you can take a number of basic steps to raise your credit score. First, ensure that payments are made on time. When payments are past due, it not only has a negative impact on your score, but new creditors will be reluctant to lend while you are delinquent on other accounts.

Being smart about taking on debt is another key factor in keeping your credit score high. As someone who is just starting off in the financial world, there will be multiple offers to open accounts, say, for an introductory credit card or short-term loan. You may also find that as your score increases, you will receive offers for larger and larger loans. (Predatory lenders are a scourge on the young as well as the old.) But just because banks are offering you those loans doesn't make them a good idea. Instead, you should only take on debt you know you can pay back in a reasonable amount of time.

Lastly, keep an eye on unpaid student loans, medical bills, and parking tickets, all of which can take a negative toll on your credit score. In fact, your credit score will take a major hit from any bill that's sent to a collection agency, so it's in your best interest to avoid letting bills get to that point. Many organizations will agree to keep bills away from collection agencies if you set up a fee payment system.

Answer the following questions based on the information provided in the article.

21. What is the range of credit scores?

22. What three items do companies keep track of to create your credit report?

23. According to the reading, for what two purposes do banks use credit scores?

24. What three other institutions use credit scores?

25. What are two problems people might have if they have no credit?

Questions 26 – 30: Match the activity to the impact it has on credit scores. You may or may not fill up each column.

WHAT RAISES YOUR CREDIT SCORE?	WHAT LOWERS YOUR CREDIT SCORE?
26.	29.
27.	30.
28.	

- ensuring bills are paid on time
- taking on debt you know you can pay back
- having bills sent to a collection agency
- setting up a fee payment system
- accepting multiple offers to open accounts

NASA Finds Good News on Forests and Carbon Dioxide

The following passage is adapted from an article entitled "NASA Finds Good News on Forests and Carbon Dioxide," published online by the National Aeronautics and Space Administration in December 2014.

A new NASA-led study shows that tropical forests may be absorbing far more carbon dioxide than many scientists thought, in response to rising atmospheric levels of greenhouse gas. The study estimates that tropical forests absorb 1.4 billion metric tons of carbon dioxide out of a total global absorption of 2.5 billion—more than is absorbed by forests in Canada, Siberia, and other northern regions, called boreal forests.

"This is good news, because uptake in boreal forests is already slowing, while tropical forests may continue to take up carbon for many years," said David Schimel of NASA's Jet Propulsion Laboratory, Pasadena, California. Schimel is lead author of a paper on the new research, appearing online today in the Proceedings of National Academy of Sciences.

Forests and other land vegetation currently remove up to 30 percent of human carbon dioxide emissions from the atmosphere during photosynthesis. If the rate of absorption were to slow down, the rate of global warming would speed up in return.

The new study is the first to devise a way to make apples-to-apples comparisons of carbon dioxide estimates from many sources at different scales: computer models of ecosystem processes, atmospheric models run backward in time to deduce the sources of today's concentrations (called inverse models), satellite images, data from experimental forest plots, and more. The researchers reconciled all types of analyses and assessed the accuracy of the results based on how well they reproduced independent, ground-based measurements. They obtained their new estimate of the tropical carbon absorption from the models they determined to be the most trusted and verified.

"Until our analysis, no one had successfully completed a global reconciliation of information about carbon dioxide effects from the atmospheric, forestry, and modeling communities," said co-author Joshua Fisher of JPL. "It is incredible that all these different types of independent data sources start to converge on an answer."

The question of which type of forest is the bigger carbon absorber "is not just an accounting curiosity," said co-author Britton Stephens of the National Center for Atmospheric Research, Boulder, Colorado. "It has big implications for our understanding of whether global terrestrial ecosystems might continue to offset our carbon dioxide emissions or might begin to exacerbate climate change."

As human-caused emissions add more carbon dioxide to the atmosphere, forests worldwide are using it to grow faster, reducing the amount that stays airborne. This effect is called carbon fertilization. "All else being equal, the effect is stronger at higher temperatures, meaning it will be higher in the tropics than in the boreal forests," Schimel said.

But climate change also decreases water availability in some regions and makes Earth warmer, leading to more frequent and larger wildfires. In the tropics, humans compound the problem by burning wood during deforestation. Fires don't just stop carbon absorption by killing trees; they also spew huge amounts of carbon into the atmosphere as the wood burns.

For about twenty-five years, most computer climate models have been showing that mid-latitude forests in the Northern Hemisphere absorb more carbon than tropical forests. That result was initially based on the then-current understanding of global air flows and limited data suggesting that deforestation was causing tropical forests to release more carbon dioxide than they were absorbing.

In the mid-2000s, Stephens used measurements of carbon dioxide made from aircraft to show that many climate models were not correctly representing flows of carbon above ground level. Models that matched the aircraft measurements better showed more carbon absorption in the tropical forests. However, there were still not enough global data sets to validate the idea of a large tropical-forest absorption. Schimel said that their new study took advantage of a great deal of work other scientists have done since Stephens' paper to pull together national and regional data of various kinds into robust, global data sets.

Schimel noted that their paper reconciles results at every scale from the pores of a single leaf, where photosynthesis takes place, to the whole Earth, as air moves carbon dioxide around the globe. "What we've had up till this paper was a theory of carbon dioxide fertilization based on phenomena at the microscopic scale and observations at the global scale that appeared to contradict those phenomena. Here, at least, is a hypothesis that provides a consistent explanation that includes both how we know photosynthesis works and what's happening at the planetary scale."

Glossary

greenhouse gas: gases that contribute to climate change and global warming

boreal forest: forest in taiga, sub-arctic areas, that feature conifer, or evergreen trees

tropical forest: forest in equatorial or sub-tropical areas; feature palm and similar trees

vegetation: plant life

carbon dioxide emissions: carbon waste products that contribute to global warming

photosynthesis: the process of turning light into energy

apples-to-apples comparisons: valid, realistic comparisons (an idiomatic expression)

deforestation: cutting and/or burning down forests, usually to create farmland

hypothesis: theory or assumption that can be tested

reconcile: bring together

Do the following statements agree with the information given in the text?

For questions 1 – 10 on your answer sheet, write:

- TRUE if the statement agrees with the information
- FALSE if the statement contradicts the information
- UNCERTAIN if there is no information on this

31. Scientists believe that tropical forests absorb more carbon dioxide than boreal forests.
32. Forests and other plants already remove a large percentage of human carbon dioxide emissions from the atmosphere.
33. Carbon fertilization is when forests use human-caused emissions in the atmosphere to grow faster.
34. Climate change decreases wildfires.
35. People burning wood in tropical areas cause fires that add to carbon emissions.

36. Until recently, scientists believed that northern forests absorbed more carbon dioxide than tropical forests.

37. Computer models from the past few decades showed that tropical forests absorbed carbon dioxide.

38. In the early 2000s, scientists discovered that computer models were not working correctly.

39. The new studies are more comprehensive than previous studies on carbon emissions absorption.

40. Tropical forests will continue to absorb carbon emissions for years to come.

WRITING

Writing Task One

You should spend about twenty minutes on this task.

This graph shows the number of months with three or fewer inches of rainfall over a six-year period in three US cities.

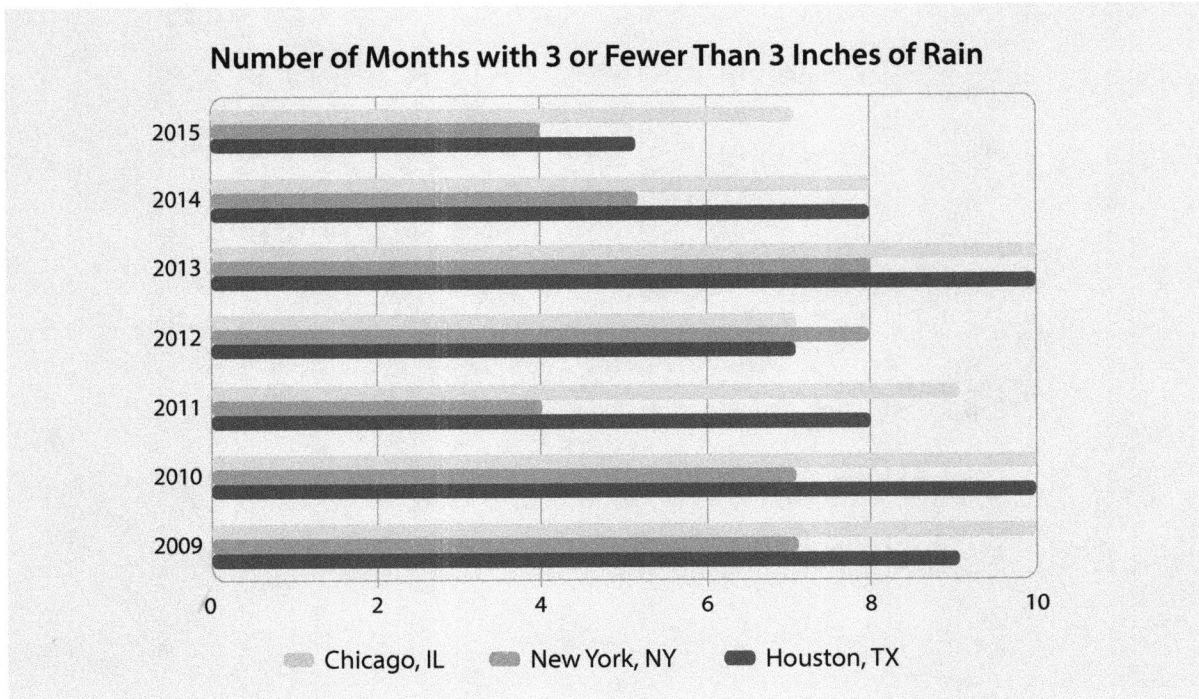

Number of Months with 3 or Fewer Than 3 Inches of Rain

Summarize the information by selecting and reporting the main features and making comparisons where relevant. Write at least 150 words.

Writing Task Two

You should spend about 40 minutes on this task.

Rapid economic growth is not at odds with smart urban development. Some of the most important economic and natural resources of the world are located in areas vulnerable to storms and flooding; however, with the right planning and investment, economic growth can continue safely and affordably.

Can cities grow in areas threatened by climate change, flooding, and storms?

In your essay, take a position on this question. Give reasons for your answer and include any relevant examples from your own knowledge or experience. Write at least 250 words.

ANSWER KEY

LISTENING

Dialogue One

Raul and Mae are talking about their experiences at different study groups.

Raul: Do you go to a philosophy study group?

Mae: Yeah; I go to the one on Wednesday nights in Room B 100 and the one on Monday nights in Room C 120.

Raul: Do they help you? What did you score on the midterm exam?

Mae: Well . . . it helps me to talk about different philosophers with other people. Since the class is mostly lecture, the study groups help me through the discussion. I can also ask questions. I feel too embarrassed to ask questions in class. Plus . . . he talks so fast! I got a B+ on the midterm, though.

Raul: Professor Roberts definitely speaks pretty fast. I've been going to the study group on Sunday night . . . and sometimes the one on Saturday morning. Neither are very good.

Mae: Why not? Do the TAs run them . . . or someone else?

Raul: The one on Sunday nights is run by a TA. It's just that it doesn't really help me. It's mostly the same as the class lecture. The one on Saturday mornings is just a group of students. Most of the time, I know more than they do about philosophy!

Mae: You should try the Monday night study group. It meets at either 6:30 or 7:00, depending on what time the TA can get there that week. Usually, anywhere from three to ten people come; most times, there are at least five of us. But I'm sure they would welcome more . . . especially if you know what you are talking about when it comes to philosophy!

Raul: I wouldn't say I *always* know what I'm talking about!

1. **Mondays**

2. **Wednesdays**

   Mae says, "I go to the one on Wednesday nights in Room B 100 and the one on Monday nights in Room C 120."

3. **discussion**

4. **questions**

   Mae says, "Since the class is mostly lecture, the study groups help me through discussion. I can also ask questions."

5. **Saturday**

6. **Sunday**

   Raul says, "I've been going to the study group on Sunday night . . . and sometimes the one on Saturday morning."

7. **Sunday night**

8. **Monday night**

   Mae says, "You should try the Monday night study group. It meets at either 6:30 or 7:00, depending on what time the TA can get there that week." Raul says, "The one on Sunday nights is run by a TA." Mae mentions going to a group on Wednesday nights, but it is not clear if a TA runs that group. Raul states, "The one on Saturday mornings is just a group of students"— with no TA.

9. **6:30**

10. **7:00**

    Mae says, "It meets at either 6:30 or 7:00."

Monologue One

Good morning. My name is Regina Cantor, and I am the director of education at Hillside Driving Academy. I'm going to speak with you briefly about the process of becoming a licensed driver in the state of Texas.

There are two situations that you might find yourself in: you might already have a license from another country, or you may have no driver's license at all. In either case, the staff here will help you.

If you have a license from another country, we will first check to see if the country of issue has a reciprocal relationship with the United States. If it does, then you will simply need to provide certain documents and pass a written test. If it doesn't, then the process might be a little more complicated, but at the most, you will need to participate in sixty hours of driver training and pass a written test. We actually encourage *everyone* to sign up for the sixty-hour training course. It covers rules of the road that are specific to the United States as well as safety laws in Texas and costs either $250 or $350, depending on whether you want to add the four hours of road training.

If you do not have a license from another country, you will go through the entire process of learning to drive with us. This will include classroom or online training, behind-the-wheel training, and a probationary period during which you will have a permit to drive with another qualified, licensed driver.

In either case, Hillside Driving Academy is here for you. We will guide you through the entire process and make sure you become a confident, licensed driver as quickly as possible. If there are no questions, I will go ahead and move on to a tour of our facility.

11. **B) is correct.** The third paragraph explains that the US has a reciprocal relationship with some countries and does not require individuals from these countries to complete driver training.

12. **A) is correct.** Regina says in the first paragraph that she is the director of education for Hillside Driving Academy.

13. **C) is correct.** Regina says the course "covers rules of the road that are specific to the United States as well as safety laws in Texas."

14. **C) is correct.** Regina says the course "covers rules of the road that are specific to the United States as well as safety laws in Texas and costs either $250 or $350, depending on whether you want to add the four hours of road training."

15. **A) is correct.** The speaker says, "If you have a license from another country, we will first check to see if the country of issue has a reciprocal relationship with the United States. If it does, then you will simply need to provide certain documents and pass a written test."

16. **C) is correct.** According to the speaker, a permit allows you to "drive with another qualified, licensed driver."

17. **C) is correct.** Regina says, "This will include classroom or online training, behind-the-wheel training, and a probationary period during which you will have a permit to drive with another qualified, licensed driver."

18. **A) is correct.** The speaker makes clear that the license will be issued from the state of Texas.

19. **B) is correct.** The speaker says that the process "will include classroom or online training."

20. **A) is correct.** Regina says, "If there are no questions, I will go ahead and move on to a tour of our facility."

Dialogue Two

A new student is speaking with an upperclassman about the different types of English classes available at the university.

Leila: Go ahead and ask me anything. I'm in my last semester as an English major. I've probably taken most of these classes.

Gavin: There are just so many classes. I never know which ones are best for me. Which kinds of English classes were your favorite?

Leila: I liked the poetry classes, especially the one about English Romantic poets. Those were pretty straightforward, and as long as I went to class and did the reading, I did well in those. I also liked the classes in literary criticism, but they are quite hard. You have to really know your stuff to get an A.

Gavin: What about writing classes?

Leila: Well, there is Basic Rhetoric and Composition—not sure who's teaching that this year. It's pretty simple, and I'm sure you've already registered for that. Then there's Technical Writing with Dr. Peters. I'd really recommend you take that since I learned a lot in that class. There's Creative Writing as well, also taught by Dr. Peters. It's a great class, especially if you enjoy reading your work out loud.

Gavin: I've registered for Rhetoric and Comp. . . . Writing is one of my hobbies, so those classes sound great! I saw a class called *Shakespearean Media* that I can take as a freshman. I also saw some other classes with interesting titles, like *Medieval Vision Literature* and *Chaucer's Life and Literature.*

Leila: The Shakespeare class focuses on the way the plays have been contextualized in modern media, such as film. That's a great class to take if you like watching movies!

Gavin: I'm not a big movie fan. I probably won't take that.

Leila: *Medieval Vision Literature* is also taught by Dr. Peters. It contains a lot of allusions to Catholic Christianity and is really interesting.

Gavin: That sounds awesome!

Leila: The class on Chaucer is taught by Dr. Summers, Chair of the English department. I've never taken it personally, but I have friends who've told me that it is a good class to take if you want to get a letter of recommendation for grad school. Dr. Summers writes many of those.

ANSWERS

21. C) is correct. Gavin never says anything about this class, so he may or may not take it.

22 C) is correct. Gavin never says anything about these classes, so he may or may not take them.

23. A) is correct. Gavin says, "I've registered for Rhetoric and Comp [. . .]."

24. A) is correct. Gavin says, "Writing is one of my hobbies, so those classes sound great!"

25. B) is correct. Gavin says, "I'm not a big movie fan. I probably won't take that."

26. A) is correct. When Leila describes *Medieval Vision Literature*, Gavin replies, "That sounds awesome!"

27. C) is correct. Gavin never says anything about this class, so he may or may not take it.

28. A) is correct. Leila says, "*Medieval Vision Literature* is also taught by Dr. Peters."

29. B) is correct. Leila says, "The class on Chaucer is taught by Dr. Summers."

30. C) is correct. Leila says, "Well, there is Basic Rhetoric and Composition—not sure who's teaching that this year."

Monologue Two

Here at the career services office, we want to help you get a job or internship that will help advance your future career. Here's what I can offer you as the best advice I have, though I, of course, have no magic formula!

The first thing I would say is to get a job or internship early—preferably in your first year of school. It is important to focus on academics, but having a job early shows future employers that you started building your work skills early on. A first job or college internship, however, should still allow time for classes. You want a role that is less than ten hours per week.

A job is nice because you will get paid for sure; some internships are unpaid. Unpaid internships aren't ideal, but they can still be helpful if they build work skills. Also, some unpaid internships do one day turn into paid jobs.

When you choose a job or internship, think about the future. Don't choose a job ONLY because the pay seems really good or because you have friends who work there. Choose a job based only on its fit for you. (Of course, if your friends work there and the job is a good fit, go ahead!)

Some jobs aren't really a good fit because they don't help you build work skills. For example, dog sitting or house sitting for family or friends doesn't look as good on a resume as a job for an actual company.

Work hours are important. It is best to avoid jobs with late hours while you are taking daytime classes. It is also very, very important to provide your employer with a copy of your class schedule and avoid full-time jobs while in school.

ANSWERS

31. A) is correct. The speaker says, "The first thing I would say is to get a job or internship early—preferably in your first year of school."

32. C) is correct. The speaker says, "A first job or college internship, however, should still allow time for classes. You want a role that is less than ten hours per week."

33. B) is correct. The speaker says, "Unpaid internships aren't ideal, but they can still be helpful if they build work skills. Also, some unpaid internships do one day turn into paid jobs."

34. A) is correct. According to the speaker, "You want a role that is less than ten hours per week."

35. A) is correct. The speaker says, "Choose a job based only on its fit for you."

36. B) is correct. The speaker says, "Don't choose a job ONLY because the pay seems really good or because you have friends who work there. Choose a job based only on its fit for you. (Of course, if your friends work there and the job is a good fit, go ahead!)"

37. C) is correct. According to the speaker, "dog sitting or house sitting for family or friends doesn't look as good on a resume as a job for an actual company."

38. C) is correct. Again, the speaker states that "dog sitting or house sitting for family or friends doesn't look as good on a resume as a job for an actual company."

39. C) is correct. The speaker says, "It is best to avoid jobs with late hours while you are taking daytime classes."

40. A) is correct. According to the speaker, "It is also very, very important to provide your employer with a copy of your class schedule."

1. the energy needs of a thirty-five-year-old woman who weighs 135 pounds: **C)**

2. the definition of a micronutrient: **B)**

3. how many calories an elderly, bedridden woman might need per pound of body weight: **C)**

4. the definition of a macronutrient: **B)**

5. whether the process of healing requires a lot of energy: **D)**

6. adequate nutrition

7. different

8. micronutrients and macronutrients

9. carbohydrates, fats, and proteins

10. vitamins and elements

11. more

12. 1800

13. 2000

14. 1150

15. **True.** In the fourth paragraph, the article says that "many patients, bedridden or otherwise, have hidden energy needs. The process of healing can be extremely energy intensive…"

16. **True.** In the fourth paragraph, the article says, "Patients on a low-energy diet may also develop deficiencies in micronutrients if the quality of their meals is not monitored closely."

17. Paragraph A	Patient Nutrition and Facility Responsibility
18. Paragraph B	Micro Versus Macro: The Basics of Nutrition
19. Paragraph C	Different Patients Have Different Needs
20. Paragraph D	Hidden Energy Needs Make a Difference

21. 300 – 850

22. loans, credit cards, bill payments

23. to decide whether to hand out loans; to determine the terms of the loan

24. car dealers, landlords, credit card companies

25. low credit limits; high interest rates

WHAT RAISES YOUR CREDIT SCORE?	WHAT LOWERS YOUR CREDIT SCORE?
26) ensuring bills are paid on time	29) having bills sent to a collection agency
27) taking on debt you know you can pay back	30) accepting multiple offers to open accounts
28) setting up a fee payment system	

31. **True.** In the first paragraph, the article states that the "study estimates that tropical forests absorb 1.4 billion metric tons of carbon dioxide out of a total global absorption of 2.5 billion—more than is absorbed by forests in Canada, Siberia, and other northern regions, called boreal forests."

32. **True.** According to the article, "Forests and other land vegetation currently remove up to 30 percent of human carbon dioxide emissions from the atmosphere during photosynthesis."

33. **True.** According to the article, "As human-caused emissions add more carbon dioxide to the atmosphere, forests worldwide are using it to grow faster, reducing the amount that stays airborne. This effect is called carbon fertilization."

34. **False.** The article states that "climate change also decreases water availability in some regions and makes Earth warmer, leading to more frequent and larger wildfires."

35. **True.** The article says, "In the tropics, humans compound the problem by burning wood during deforestation. Fires don't just stop carbon absorption by killing trees; they also spew huge amounts of carbon into the atmosphere as the wood burns."

36. **True.** According to the article, "For about twenty-five years, most computer climate models have been showing that mid-latitude forests in the Northern Hemisphere absorb more carbon than tropical forests."

37. **False.** The article states that "For about twenty-five years, most computer climate models have been showing that mid-latitude forests in the Northern Hemisphere absorb more carbon than tropical forests."

38. **True.** According to the article, "In the mid-2000s, Stephens used measurements of carbon dioxide made from aircraft to show that many climate models were not correctly representing flows of carbon above ground level."

39. **True.** The article quotes one of the authors of the study: "'Until our analysis, no one had successfully completed a global reconciliation of information about carbon dioxide effects from the atmospheric, forestry, and modeling communities,' said co-author Joshua Fisher of JPL."

40. **Uncertain.** There is no evidence in the article to support this assertion, and the article even quotes one of the authors of the study: "'uptake in boreal forests is already slowing, while tropical forests may continue to take up carbon for many years,' said David Schimel of NASA's Jet Propulsion Laboratory." Dr. Schimel says tropical forests *may* continue to take up carbon; there is no certainty that they will do so.

WRITING

Writing Task One

This bar graph illustrates the number of months in which rainfall was three inches or less for the three cities of Chicago, New York, and Houston over the period of 2009 – 2015. Units are measured in number of months.

Each of the three cities had four or more months in which rainfall was three inches or below in each of the six years. Chicago and Houston had considerably more months of lower rainfall than New York City, with two years in which they had ten months with three or fewer inches of rainfall each. These two years—2010 and 2013—along with 2009 saw the most months with three or fewer inches of rainfall for these two cities.

The months with low rainfall in Chicago remained consistent from 2009 to 2010 at ten months per year. This dipped slightly to nine months in 2011 and then dipped significantly to only seven months with three or fewer inches of rain in 2012. By 2013, Chicago was back up to ten months with three or fewer inches of rain. However, the city saw an increase in rainfall in the following two years: only eight months in 2014 had three or fewer inches, and seven months in 2015 had three or fewer inches.

In both 2009 and 2010, New York had seven months with three or fewer inches of rainfall. This dipped to only four months in 2011, then increased to eight months in 2012 and 2013. The years 2014 and 2015 were also wetter, with only five months with three or fewer inches in 2014 and four months with three or fewer inches in 2015.

Houston had nine months with three or fewer inches of rainfall in 2009 and ten dry months in 2010. The years 2011 and 2012 were wetter, with eight months of three or fewer inches and seven months of three or fewer inches of rain, respectively. The year 2013 saw ten months with low rainfall for Houston, but by 2014, this had dipped to only eight months. The year 2015 was the wettest overall for Houston, with only five months with three or fewer inches of rain.

Writing Task Two

Recent powerful storms have caused extreme destruction, especially in cities and areas where population has been growing rapidly. But these growing centers of population power the national economies of global industrial powers. We cannot just abandon cities where hurricanes, cyclones, and typhoons strike. Economic development and growth can continue. Governments can secure communities using lessons learned from past tragedies. The solution is to encourage investment in urban planning and public safety.

Before growing cities get even larger, governments must take action to prevent the growth of slums, improve existing infrastructure for cities (or develop new infrastructure), and establish good urban management policies. In addition, the private sector can sponsor urban development and safety.

In the United States, the Gulf Coast area contains oil and gas resources and major ports. Securing the coastal areas is a smart investment. Farther north, New York City and its region are an important part of the world economy. Both areas are central to global markets and vulnerable to storms and flooding. Slowing any growth in these areas would damage the global financial and fossil fuel markets.

Fast-growing South and Southeast Asia—the Philippines, Bangladesh, Myanmar, Vietnam, Malaysia, and Indonesia—are vulnerable to storms. So are Taiwan, Hong Kong, and parts of India. These places are also home to the factories and workers who produce many of the world's consumer products. Slowing development would hurt these countries. Millions of people would lose jobs and opportunities.

Today, there are more ways than ever to develop products and procedures to ensure safety. Cities can establish evacuation routes and procedures. NGOs can distribute survival items during storm seasons. Technology can warn residents about dangerous conditions, giving them time to prepare and making it possible to live in storm-prone areas more safely.

While storms and other natural disasters will remain a threat to human life, we cannot stop all economic activity. Thanks to cooperation and innovation, countries can protect communities as they drive the economic growth of those regions affected by major storms. That way, development can continue in as safe an environment as possible.

www.ingramcontent.com/pod-product-compliance
Lightning Source LLC
Chambersburg PA
CBHW062054090426
42740CB00016B/3128